Managing Negative Emotions Without Drinking

Managing Negative Emotions Without Drinking is the ideal companion to *Emotion Regulation Treatment of Alcohol Use Disorders*. Each of the 12 individual weekly treatment sessions presents scientifically tested strategies for managing emotions without alcohol, including mindfulness practices, direct experiencing of emotion, and cognitive and behavioral skills to manage high-risk drinking situations and prevent relapse to alcohol use. The step-by-step exercises, user-friendly worksheets, and in-session and between-session skill practice help clients gain a basic understanding of the role that emotions play in harmful alcohol use and assist you in developing the skills needed to manage these emotions and cravings without alcohol.

Paul R. Stasiewicz, PhD, is a licensed clinical psychologist as well as senior research scientist and director of the Addiction Treatment Services outpatient clinic at the University at Buffalo's Research Institute on Addictions. His NIH-funded research focuses on the development of novel behavioral therapies for alcohol use disorders.

Clara M. Bradizza, PhD, is a senior research scientist at the Research Institute on Addictions and a research scientist in the Department of Family Medicine at the University at Buffalo. Her research, funded by NIH, includes the development of innovative affect-based interventions for both alcohol and smoking. Dr. Bradizza is a member of the University at Buffalo (UB) Institutional Review Board and is a grant reviewer at the National Institutes of Health.

Kim S. Slosman, MS, LMHC, is a clinical research project d at the Research Institute on Addictions at the University at Buffalo with clinical practice and supervision experience in mental health has experience developing and delivering manualized treatm a therapist on four previous clinical trials involving emotion regulation training substance-abusing clients.

D1126833

Managing Negative Emotions Without Drinking

A Workbook of Effective Strategies

Paul R. Stasiewicz

Clara M. Bradizza

Kim S. Slosman

Routledge
Taylor & Francis Group

NEW YORK AND LONDON

First published 2018
by Routledge
711 Third Avenue, New York, NY 10017

and by Routledge
2 Park Square, Milton Park, Abingdon, Oxon, OX14 4RN

Routledge is an imprint of the Taylor & Francis Group, an informa business

© 2018 Paul R. Stasiewicz, Clara M. Bradizza, Kim S. Slosman

The right of Paul R. Stasiewicz, Clara M. Bradizza, Kim S. Slosman
to be identified as authors of this work has been asserted by them in
accordance with sections 77 and 78 of the Copyright, Designs and
Patents Act 1988.

Library of Congress Cataloging-in-Publication Data
A catalog record for this book has been requested

ISBN: 978-1-138-21587-0 (hbk)
ISBN: 978-1-138-21588-7 (pbk)
ISBN: 978-1-315-40586-5 (ebk)

Typeset in ACaslon
by Apex CoVantage, LLC

The best way out is always through.

—Robert Frost

To our children, Adam and Hannah, who have helped us to become more
patient and to value being present in the moment.
Paul R. Stasiewicz & Clara M. Bradizza

To my husband, Aaron, and my children, Mike and Kaiti,
for their love, laughter, and never-failing support.
Kim S. Slosman

Contents

Acknowledgments

We would like to give a special thanks to our colleagues Dr. Scott Coffey, Dr. Gregory Gudleski, and Dr. Suzy Bird Gulliver, who shared their knowledge, expertise, and friendship as we developed Emotion Regulation Treatment (ERT) of Alcohol Use Disorders. We are grateful to all of the clients and to the therapists who have provided us with extremely insightful feedback through various revisions and improvements to the treatment manual.

Numerous project staff including project directors, data analysts, research assistants, consultants, and colleagues have all made important contributions to this work. Our thanks go to Dr. Kenneth E. Leonard and Dr. Gerard J. Connors for contributing institutional resources that helped to support the clinical research studies on which ERT is based.

Lastly, this work would not have been possible without the generous support and funding from the National Institute on Alcohol Abuse and Alcoholism (R01 AA15064, R21 AA017115; PI: Stasiewicz; and R01 AA024628; MPI: Stasiewicz/ Bradizza), National Institute on Drug Abuse (R01 DA021802; PI: Bradizza), and the Office of Research on Women's Health at the National Institutes of Health.

About the Authors

Paul R. Stasiewicz, PhD, is a senior research scientist at the Research Institute on Addictions (RIA) at the University at Buffalo. He received his PhD in clinical psychology from the University at Binghamton. He conducts clinical research on the development and evaluation of novel behavioral therapies for substance use disorders. Dr. Stasiewicz has been the director of the Alcohol Treatment Service, the outpatient treatment clinic at RIA, for over 20 years. His research is funded by the National Institutes of Health and his research interests include understanding the role of craving, emotions, and learning-based processes in the development and maintenance of alcohol use disorders.

Clara M. Bradizza, PhD, is a senior research scientist at the Research Institute on Addictions at the University at Buffalo. She received her PhD in clinical psychology from the University at Binghamton. Her research has been funded by the National Institutes of Health and includes the development and testing of innovative affect-based interventions for both alcohol and smoking. In addition, much of her clinical research has focused on vulnerable populations including pregnant smokers and individuals dually diagnosed with a serious mental illness and a substance use disorder.

Kim S. Slosman, MS, LMHC, is a clinical research project director at the Research Institute on Addictions at the University at Buffalo with more than 20 years of clinical practice and supervision experience in mental health and addiction. She received her MS in Rehabilitation Counseling from the University at Buffalo. She has worked in community mental health, private practice, and clinical research settings, including providing clinical supervision for a number of studies funded by the National Institutes of Health. Her interest areas include alcohol-use disorders, mindfulness, executive functioning, and Motivational Interviewing.

Chapter 1

Introduction

What Is Alcohol Use Disorder?

Alcohol use disorder (AUD) involves continued use of alcohol despite experiencing significant alcohol-related problems. As shown in Table 1, people with AUD have four major types of symptoms that correspond to:

- Impaired control
- Social impairment
- Risky use
- Pharmacological criteria

AUDs range in severity from mild to severe, with severity based on the number of symptom criteria that are endorsed. Changes in severity can occur over time as reflected by decreases or increases in the frequency or amount of alcohol use and alcohol-related problems. If two or more of the symptoms occur within a 12-month period, and result in significant impairment or distress, then this program, a combination of cognitive-behavioral therapy (CBT) for alcohol dependence and Emotion Regulation Treatment (ERT), can help.

What Is an Emotion?

The word *emotion* is derived from the Latin verb *movere*, to move. Simply stated, emotions provide a source of motivation for behavior; they move us to action. In the case of negative emotions—a focus of this treatment—they are experienced as unpleasant, unwanted, or aversive, and typically motivate us to act in ways that will

TABLE 1 Symptoms of Alcohol Use Disorder

Impaired Control

1. Alcohol is often taken in larger amounts or over a longer period than was intended.
2. There is a persistent desire or unsuccessful efforts to cut down or control alcohol use.
3. A great deal of time is spent in activities necessary to obtain alcohol, use alcohol, or recover from its effects.
4. Person experiences craving, or a strong desire or urge to use alcohol.

Social Impairment

5. Recurrent alcohol use results in a failure to fulfill major role obligations at work, school, or home.
6. Alcohol use continues despite having persistent or recurrent social or interpersonal problems caused or intensified by the effects of alcohol.
7. Important social, occupational, or recreational activities are given up or reduced because of alcohol use.

Risky Use

8. Recurrent alcohol use occurs in situations in which it is physically hazardous to drink.
9. Alcohol use is continued despite knowledge of having a persistent or recurrent physical or psychological problem that is likely to have been caused or intensified by alcohol.

Pharmacological

10. Tolerance, as defined by either of the following:
    a. need for noticeably increased amounts of alcohol to achieve intoxication or the desired effect
    b. A noticeably diminished effect with continued use of the same amount of alcohol
11. Withdrawal, as demonstrated by either of the following:
    a. A known withdrawal syndrome for alcohol as indicated by two or more of the following symptoms upon stopping or reducing alcohol use that has been heavy and prolonged: autonomic hyperactivity (e.g., sweating, increased heart rate), hand tremor, insomnia, agitation, seizures, nausea or vomiting, anxiety, transient (temporary) visual, tactile, or auditory hallucinations
    b. Alcohol (or a closely related substance, such as a benzodiazepine) is taken to relieve or avoid withdrawal symptoms

Adapted from: American Psychiatric Association (2013).

reduce, terminate, or help us to avoid these emotions. In the case of positive emotions, they are experienced as pleasant or desirable and typically motivate behaviors to increase, initiate, or approach them. There are many definitions of emotion, but most include the following common elements: (1) emotions communicate information to ourselves and others to help guide our behavior so that we can pursue our goals; (2) emotions vary in intensity (from mild to intense), valence (positive or negative), duration (short or long), and whether they are primary (an initial emotional response) or secondary (an emotional response to an emotional response); (3) emotions have three components, experiential/cognitive (i.e., awareness of the response, a feeling), physiological (e.g., facial flushing, increased respiration or heart beat), and behavioral (e.g., laughter, aggression, alcohol use); and (4) emotions can be modified. Although emotional responses may arise suddenly and sometimes feel like they will never end, knowing that they can be modified gave rise to the ERT described in this workbook.

Emotions and Alcohol Use

Which emotions motivate alcohol use? Both positive and negative emotions can motivate alcohol consumption. An individual who is experiencing a positive emotion (e.g., joy, contentment) may drink to extend or enhance the positive emotional state. Drinking that occurs in celebratory social situations (e.g., a weekend barbecue with friends, a college graduation party) represents alcohol consumption that is motivated by a positive emotional state. In this case, alcohol may provide a source of positive reinforcement or reward, and increases the likelihood that the behavior will be repeated in similar situations in the future. In contrast, an individual experiencing a negative or unpleasant emotion (e.g., frustration, anxiety, irritability) may drink to reduce or stop the unpleasant feeling. In this case, alcohol provides a source of negative reinforcement or escape (i.e., reduces or removes an unpleasant emotional state) and increases the likelihood that the behavior will be repeated in similar situations in the future. Please note that in both cases—drinking for positive or negative reinforcement motives—the behavior of drinking is strengthened and maintained. Importantly, as a person moves from a pattern of nonproblem to problem use of alcohol, a shift occurs from positive reinforcement or reward drinking to negative reinforcement or escape drinking. Therefore, people with an AUD often drink to escape or avoid unpleasant or uncomfortable emotional states. In fact, unpleasant emotions are the most common reasons for drinking among people receiving treatment for an AUD. Unpleasant emotions also account for nearly 40% of relapse episodes following treatment. Included in this discussion of unpleasant emotions are the uncomfortable physical sensations that may arise when a person stops or reduces a period of heavy or prolonged drinking. Although many individuals with AUD may not experience severe withdrawal symptoms (i.e., hallucinations, seizures), milder symptoms such as increased irritability, while not identified by the person as a symptom of alcohol withdrawal, may be experienced as an uncomfortable emotional state and may be relieved by the consumption of alcohol. To the extent that alcohol use and related behaviors reduce or eliminate the unpleasant physical state, the behavior of drinking is further strengthened and maintained (i.e., negatively reinforced). In this way, through the process of positive and negative reinforcement, individuals learn to modify or regulate their emotional states by drinking.

What Is Emotion Regulation?

Like emotion, many definitions of emotion regulation have been proposed. A current definition by James Gross (1998) defines emotion regulation as the "processes by which individuals influence which emotions they have, when they have them, and how they experience and express these emotions" (p. 275). Several other features of this definition deserve discussion. First, an emotion can be regulated at different stages in its development. Strategies that are used early in the emotion-generative process are called *antecedent-focused*. An example might help to illustrate this point. A former client, we will call him "Tom," was invited to his 25th high school reunion. As the reunion drew closer, he became increasingly anxious about attending. When asked why he felt anxious, he reported having thoughts about not being very successful and concerned that his peers would find him uninteresting. He imagined going to the reunion, standing alone, looking kind of awkward, and therefore standing out. As he talked about this situation his heart was beating faster and he considered not showing up to the reunion. In this example, Tom was choosing to interpret this situation in a negative way—namely, that he was uninteresting, his peers would shut him out, and he would be left standing alone with no one to talk to. That would be unpleasant for most anyone! In order to help Tom understand his emotions, his therapist worked with him to understand how he was interpreting the situation. In this case, Tom's appraisal of the reunion was very negative and this negative interpretation affected the way he felt. So, before going to the reunion, Tom's therapist worked with him to develop alternative ways of interpreting the situation. We call this *Cognitive Reappraisal;* that is, Tom was thinking only of the worst-case scenario, which was still in the realm of possibility, but certainly not the only possible outcome. By acknowledging alternative possible interpretations (e.g., "Even if one person finds me uninteresting, certainly not everyone will." "Other people that I have met have found me interesting."), Tom was able to effectively decrease his anxiety to manageable levels *before* attending the reunion. This is why Cognitive Reappraisal is called an *antecedent-focused emotion regulation strategy*. You will learn more about Cognitive Reappraisal in Session 4 of this treatment. Alternatives to antecedent-focused strategies are response-focused strategies, which are used to regulate an ongoing emotion. Deep breathing when a person is experiencing increased anxiety is an example of a response-focused strategy—the person is trying to regulate an emotion they are currently experiencing.

A second feature of the definition of emotion regulation is that emotion regulatory strategies can target pleasant as well as unpleasant emotions. Although our ERT emphasizes the regulation of unpleasant emotions by drinking, drinking can also regulate pleasant emotions. For example, a person who drinks while watching a football game with friends may experience greater social pleasure. Finally, it's important to consider the purpose of emotion regulation. In the earlier example, it may seem that the individual is drinking to enhance social pleasure. However, if the individual is socially anxious, then drinking in social situations may be an attempt by the individual to regulate (that is, reduce or remove) unpleasant emotions (i.e., social anxiety). Therefore, it is important to understand the relationship between alcohol consumption and a person's reasons for using alcohol (e.g., down-regulate or reduce unpleasant emotions, or up-regulate or increase positive emotions) in specific situations. Individuals who are less skilled at emotion regulation may resort to a range of unhealthy behaviors, including excessive alcohol use, in an attempt to help regulate unpleasant emotions that they experience as unbearable.

What Is Emotion Regulation Treatment?

Emotion Regulation Treatment (ERT) combines a set of clinical strategies that have been adapted from current therapies that have been found to help clients develop skills to regulate unpleasant emotions in healthy ways. Although some of these treatment techniques may be unfamiliar to you right now, they will be explained in treatment and you will have an opportunity to ask questions and practice them over the course of treatment. Specific strategies adapted for use in ERT include behavioral analysis of drinking situations involving unpleasant emotions including situations in which you are with other people and those in which you are alone, and training in behavioral coping skills that help people manage their emotions. You will work with your therapist to learn mindfulness-based cognitive strategies in which you will learn the process of observing and experiencing emotion, designed to increase attention to the present moment and to experience the emotion without judgment or avoidance. Finally, you will work collaboratively with your therapist to develop unpleasant emotional imagery scenes taken from situations in your daily life that are associated with drinking. These imagery scenes will be used in the direct experiencing of emotion sessions as a way to increase your acceptance and tolerance of uncomfortable feelings and physical sensations that often lead to drinking. The goal of these direct experiencing of emotion sessions is to help you manage these types of unpleasant emotional situations in your daily life without alcohol.

ERT places a greater emphasis on emotion regulation strategies than other cognitive-behavioral treatments for changing drinking behavior. ERT is designed to help individuals regulate both pleasant and unpleasant emotions that often motivate alcohol use. With its emphasis on attention to the present-moment experience (i.e., the "here and now"), ERT provides additional skills for dealing with drinking triggers, especially emotional drinking triggers. The skills that are taught in ERT enable a person with AUD to cope with unpleasant emotions or uncomfortable physical sensations without reacting to them by drinking. Although effective use of these emotion regulation skills can improve alcohol treatment outcomes, the CBT component of the ERT treatment program provides important skills for achieving and maintaining abstinence from alcohol (e.g., drink refusal skills, coping with urges and cravings). Thus, the ERT program is a combination of emotion regulation skills and CBT coping skills that work together to help individuals with AUD to achieve and maintain abstinence from alcohol.

How Was the Program Developed?

ERT was developed by the authors at the Research Institute on Addictions at the University at Buffalo. During development of ERT, changes and refinements of different versions of the treatment manual were completed by the authors and were based on both oral and written feedback from expert consultants, therapists conducting the treatment sessions, and the clients themselves. For example, clients responded to questions about what was helpful during the treatment sessions, whether the session content was clear, and how the session content could be made more helpful; they also provided an overall rating of the session (1 = Poor or Not Helpful to 7 = Excellent or Very Helpful). Based on therapist and client feedback, the manual was revised and the process was repeated. After delivering the treatment to different groups of clients, the manual was again revised based on client and therapist feedback. The final version of the treatment manual was evaluated in a larger treatment study of people with AUD. The results of this study demonstrated the ability to train therapists to administer ERT, excellent client satisfaction with the treatment, and that the treatment was effective in reducing alcohol use among individuals with AUD.

What Are the Benefits and Risks of This Program?

Benefits

ERT was developed to enhance standard CBT for AUD. Thirty years of research on CBT has consistently demonstrated its effectiveness as a treatment for AUD. To this effective CBT treatment, ERT adds emotion regulation strategies taken from existing interventions that address a range of mental health disorders—such as anxiety, posttraumatic stress disorder (PTSD), and depression—including AUDs. Although there is evidence that standard treatments for AUD, like CBT, result in reductions in unpleasant emotions (e.g., Brown & Schuckit, 1988; Brown, Irwin, & Schuckit, 1991; Witkiewitz, Bowen, & Donovan, 2011), the addition of emotion regulation strategies to standard CBT in our study resulted in greater reductions in unpleasant emotions and better alcohol treatment outcomes for individuals with AUD.

Risks

The major risks associated with ERT are experiencing uncomfortable emotions and urges or cravings to drink alcohol, especially when participating in the imagery scenes during treatment (Sessions 7–10). ERT is designed to address the problem of drinking in response to uncomfortable emotions including urges and cravings by having you directly experience those feelings while also learning specific skills to help you regulate your emotions and cravings in healthy ways. Because the experience of unpleasant emotions and cravings can be difficult, especially at first, it is recommended that you do ERT with the help and guidance of your therapist.

Although this is not a risk per se, it's important to differentiate ERT from other treatments that use similar treatment techniques to treat symptoms of PTSD and several other anxiety disorders. ERT is not a treatment for these disorders and is not intended to help people with trauma-related problems. Although AUD and PTSD frequently occur together, there are several integrated treatments that have been specifically developed to help people who have both an alcohol or drug use disorder and PTSD (Back et al., 2015; Coffey et al., 2016; for a review see Torchalla, Nosen, Rostam, & Allen, 2012).

The Role of Medications

Medications for AUD, when used in combination with behavioral treatment, can reduce cravings and other symptoms of AUD. There are three medications approved by the U.S. Food and Drug Administration (FDA) for use in treating AUD. Acamprosate is a medication that has been shown to help individuals who have achieved abstinence to maintain abstinence for an extended period of time. Naltrexone, a medication that blocks the effects of opioids, has been used effectively to reduce craving for alcohol among people who are trying to quit drinking. Disulfiram (Antabuse) is a medication that changes the way the body metabolizes alcohol, resulting in an unpleasant reaction that can include flushing, nausea, and other unpleasant symptoms if a person takes the medication and then consumes alcohol. People who are already taking one of these medications for AUD may still benefit from ERT.

It is common for people entering AUD treatment to be taking prescribed medication for the treatment of an anxiety or mood disorder. Someone who is already taking a medication for anxiety or depression, and who also suffers from AUD, can stay on the medication and go through the ERT program. However, these individuals are encouraged to continue seeing their prescribing physician for medication monitoring and let them know they are receiving treatment for an AUD.

In the next chapter, we will provide you with information regarding who is most likely to benefit from ERT; how cravings and emotions work together to promote drinking, and how ERT works to separate unpleasant emotions and craving for alcohol; and the importance of practicing skills and strategies that you can use to get through high-risk drinking situations without drinking.

Chapter 2

Is This Treatment Right for You?

Drinking in Situations Involving Unpleasant or Pleasant Emotions

Emotions are short-term responses to particular situations or events. People feel joyful when holding a newborn, lonely when they lose a long-time companion, angry when they feel they have been wronged by someone. Both pleasant (e.g., joy, contentment) and unpleasant (e.g., anger, fear, sadness) emotions are often reported as reasons for drinking heavily. People with AUD may drink to increase their experience of positive emotions or decrease their experience of unpleasant emotions. Most people with AUD report drinking in response to both types of emotions, although drinking heavily in response to unpleasant emotions usually occurs much more frequently. In addition, among people who are trying to remain abstinent, up to 40% of relapse episodes are reported to occur in situations involving unpleasant emotions. This figure rises to 75% when we take into account situations that involve other people such as those where people experience social pressure to drink or conflict with others (Baker, Morse, & Sherman, 1987). People who report drinking in response to pleasant emotions may drink when they feel relaxed such as when on vacation and free of their usual responsibilities. Others may say they drink in order to relax, escape, or take the "edge" off. Some report drinking in social celebratory situations in order to enhance their experience of pleasure. Finally, there are people who view drinking alcohol as a "reward" for tolerating or putting up with a situation that is uncomfortable, boring, or annoying. In the short term, alcohol use can provide some benefits in each of those situations. But if you have picked up this workbook, you most likely know that in the long run, excessive alcohol use does not solve problems and often makes things worse.

Who Can Benefit from ERT?

We recommend treatment with ERT if:

- You are someone who frequently uses alcohol to help manage your emotions, and you have been experiencing problems as the result of your drinking (see "What Is Alcohol Use Disorder?" section in Chapter 1).
- You are open to the idea of abstinence as a treatment goal.

We do *not* recommend treatment with ERT if:

- You have experienced a past or recent trauma and are seeking treatment specifically to improve symptoms of PTSD.
- You have had multiple admissions to outpatient treatment programs for AUD and you have been unable to achieve abstinence or reduce your consumption of alcohol while in outpatient treatment. A course of inpatient treatment or detoxification may be a necessary first step before beginning ERT.
- You are unwilling to consider abstinence as your treatment goal.
- In addition to AUD, you have a serious mental illness such as schizophrenia or bipolar disorder that may require an additional or different treatment, or a greater level of monitoring.
- You have a strong desire to injure yourself or a plan to commit suicide or to harm other people. Such thoughts and behaviors do sometimes occur in people with AUD; however, if these thoughts are current and strong we recommend that you address those first in consultation with a mental health professional before beginning ERT.

If one or more of these situations is true for you, and you have doubts or concerns about whether ERT is right for you, we encourage you to discuss these concerns with your therapist and together decide on the best course of action as to how and when to proceed with ERT.

Alcohol Craving

Experts in addiction define craving as a strong desire or urge to use alcohol. Take note of the word "strong" in this definition. What is a "strong" desire or urge? It's a subjective term; that is, it's based on personal feelings, and some people with AUD may deny ever having a "strong" desire or urge to use alcohol. Does this mean they don't experience craving at all? That seems unlikely. Most people seeking treatment for AUD do report cravings or desires. It's a very common experience observed across a number of different substances of abuse (e.g., alcohol, nicotine, opiates). For those individuals who say they don't experience strong cravings, or for that matter any craving, it may be that their drinking behavior has become so efficient that they drink before the experience of craving fully develops and reaches conscious awareness. Others may not acknowledge or talk about cravings because they feel that to admit to them poses a threat to their sobriety. As one client said, "If I admit to cravings, then I might as well drink because in my mind I've already relapsed." Finally, some people are not as sensitive to their thoughts, feelings, and physical sensations as others. These people may have more difficulty identifying or labeling their experiences as a desire or urge to use alcohol; they may experience it as a "discomfort" or "pressure." During ERT, you will become more aware of what your cravings are like. You will learn to experience urges and cravings and not react to them by drinking. And finally, you will see that cravings are like waves that build, crest, and then fall away. Over time, you will become like the skilled surfer who spots the ocean swell before it becomes a wave.

Emotions and Craving

Pleasant or unpleasant emotions can provide a strong motivation to drink alcohol and they also can generate a strong urge or craving. The emotion can act as a cue for an individual that having a drink right now would feel good. Emotions and cravings usually track each other quite closely; that is, when one goes up, so does the other. Because emotions are a natural part of life, an important goal of this treatment is to break the connection between unpleasant emotions and your craving for alcohol. By learning to accept and tolerate unpleasant emotions without drinking, you will gain the ability to respond in healthier ways that do not involve alcohol. That is, you will learn alternative ways to respond when experiencing an unpleasant thought, emotion, or physical sensation.

Avoiding People, Places, and Things That Remind You of Alcohol

Early in treatment, it's a good idea to avoid certain people or places that are strong reminders of drinking, if you can. Before you try going into these high-risk situations, you should try out the skills and strategies you will learn in ERT in very low risk for drinking situations and see how they work for you. Similarly, you wouldn't want to have your very first dive into a pool to be off a 100-foot diving board—you might want to practice diving from the edge of the pool first! Although we advise taking care in deciding which high-risk situations you expose yourself to early in treatment, there are certain things associated with alcohol use that are often difficult to avoid, such as TV commercials, billboards, or driving by restaurants or bars where you used to drink. However, there are ways to manage these situations that can help you to reduce your risk of drinking and these will be discussed over the course of treatment. One of the things we ask you *not* to avoid is any unpleasant emotion associated with alcohol use. This can be difficult, especially for individuals who have used alcohol to avoid these unpleasant emotions for a long time. However, learning to experience and manage these unpleasant emotions is part of the treatment and you will have many opportunities to work with your therapist to learn to manage them without drinking alcohol.

Practice, Practice, Practice: The Importance of Working the Program

As humans we learn thousands of behaviors over the course of our lifetime. We learn to ride bikes, drive cars, add and subtract numbers, and communicate with others, to name a few. Over time, and hundreds and thousands of trials in which we practice them, our behaviors become more efficient. Once these behaviors are well-learned, they require much less effort to carry out and seem to occur without much conscious attention or even awareness on our part (i.e., driving a car, taking a shower). Alcohol use is no exception. It is a behavior that has been repeated many times and has been shaped by principles of positive (the pleasurable effects of alcohol) and negative (reduction or removal of an unpleasant or uncomfortable physical or emotional state by alcohol consumption) reinforcement. Well-learned behaviors, often called *habits,* can be difficult to change. However, we know that many people do change their behaviors. Many people with AUD change their drinking behavior. Some change on their own without the help of formal treatment. This is called *natural recovery* (Sobell, Ellingstad, & Sobell, 2000). Other people change with the help of treatment. Fortunately, there are many strategies for changing well-learned behaviors, but it takes a willingness to learn, and some effort or practice. Indeed, a key to successful behavior change is practice.

This workbook is a guide to behavior change. It includes explanations, but more importantly, it includes many helpful worksheets and practice exercises. The exercises can be modified or adapted to fit your lifestyle. The important point is that you try them out, find out what works best for you and then, Practice, Practice, Practice!

Alternative Treatments

Currently, there are no other available treatments for AUD that place as much emphasis on emotion and emotion regulation as does ERT. However, there are several excellent alternative treatments for AUD. These include Motivational Interviewing (Miller & Rollnick, 2013) and a number of cognitive-behavioral treatments for AUD that focus on learning new behaviors and skills. These treatment approaches are supported by research that shows strong evidence that they work to improve drinking outcomes (Miller, Wilbourne, & Hettema, 2003). The CBT component of ERT is an excellent stand-alone treatment for AUD, which is why we chose to include it as part of our treatment program. CBT teaches skills for managing high-risk drinking situations (e.g., Monti, Kadden, Rohsenow, Cooney, & Abrams, 2002). In numerous research studies, individuals receiving CBT have demonstrated substantial improvements in the number of days they are abstinent and also in the number or level of alcohol-related problems. Alcoholics Anonymous (AA), while not a formal treatment, can offer a valuable support network for individuals seeking to quit drinking. It's not uncommon for individuals to participate in an alcohol treatment program while at the same time attending AA meetings. An important point when selecting any treatment is that you understand and are comfortable with the approach being offered.

In the next chapter, we will provide an overview of the treatment program. We will describe the different factors that combine to maintain heavy drinking for people with AUD and how the clinical strategies in this treatment work together to help you change your drinking.

Chapter 3

Session 1

About This Treatment

Session 1 Goals

- Learn about the treatment program and the procedures that will be used.
- Learn about the connection between emotions and alcohol.
- Learn an awareness technique for becoming more aware of physical sensations.
- Learn a brief awareness technique that can be used throughout the day.

Overview of Program and Treatment Procedures Used

You have made the important decision to begin treatment to help you abstain from alcohol. This can be a stressful time as you begin thinking about the changes you may have to make in your life. However, despite the challenges that treatment will present, you will not be doing this alone. You and your therapist will work together in session to help you develop the skills and strategies to overcome your alcohol problem. These will include effective ways to manage unpleasant emotions, and cognitive and behavioral skills to manage high-risk situations.

In this program, you are going to focus on the unpleasant emotions, sensations, and urges or cravings you are experiencing, and on your difficulties managing these experiences without alcohol. The treatment program consists of twelve 90-minute sessions scheduled weekly, so the treatment will be completed in about 3 months.

The main tools of this treatment program are mindfulness, direct experiencing of emotion, and cognitive and behavioral coping skills for managing your high-risk drinking situations involving unpleasant emotions, sensations, and urges and craving to drink.

You and your therapist will discuss why this treatment is important for you and how it will be tailored to you and the specific situations related to your alcohol use. You will have the chance to ask questions and make sure you understand why this treatment is aimed at helping you find effective strategies for managing uncomfortable thoughts, emotions, and physical sensations that are related to your use of alcohol.

You are receiving this treatment because you have indicated that you sometimes drink in situations involving unpleasant emotions. You may also experience uncomfortable urges or cravings when attempting to abstain in similar situations. Some people who drink in response to unpleasant emotions tell us that they have tried and failed to resist drinking or that they didn't know another way to cope with how they were feeling. Still others have said that they thought the unpleasant emotions would continue to increase and become intolerable. Some people just cannot picture themselves doing anything other than drinking in these situations. Have you had such thoughts and experiences? If so, you are not alone. We encourage you to share these experiences with your therapist. In this session, you and your therapist will discuss how this treatment makes sense for you and the problems with alcohol you are having, and how it will be different from how you have approached your unpleasant emotions, sensations, and urges and cravings in the past.

Although many people do recover from alcohol problems, others relapse in situations involving unpleasant emotions or conflicts with others. Therefore, it is helpful for your recovery to understand how drinking in response to unpleasant emotions maintains problem alcohol use.

The first factor that maintains your problem alcohol use is the positive reinforcing effects that consuming alcohol provides. These immediate pleasant effects of alcohol consumption can make it very difficult to abstain in situations where you want to experience those pleasant or calming effects. Also, attempts to abstain in such situations can be perceived as unpleasant because you are denying yourself the positive effects of alcohol. Therefore, some people experience this as a loss of pleasure. Again, drinking in these situations only serves to prolong the problem. But to deal with the feelings of loss and what to do next, you will need something to do besides drinking. At first, it will seem like there are very few alternatives to drinking that can come close to providing you with the pleasure or relief that alcohol can provide. But, by committing to trying a different path, you will be given the opportunity to see that the uncomfortable emotions and sensations will decrease without the use of alcohol. Over time, alcohol use will no longer be viewed as one of the few solutions to managing life's unpleasant experiences. You will be learning a range of alternative activities and behaviors that can provide you with pleasurable experiences. So, over the next 12 weeks you and your therapist are going to work very hard to help you learn how to live a meaningful life without alcohol. You will experience some discomfort as you face situations without the use of alcohol, but your therapist will be there during your sessions to help guide you through.

A second factor that maintains your problem alcohol use is *avoidance* of unpleasant emotions, thoughts, sensations, urges, or cravings. The main way that people with an alcohol problem avoid dealing with these unpleasant and uncomfortable experiences is to drink. However, while the strategy of avoiding these unpleasant experiences works in the short term, in the long run it actually prolongs the unpleasant emotions and uncomfortable sensations, and prevents you from recovering. Can you think of things that you have avoided with your alcohol use? It is helpful to write them down and talk about them with your therapist.

Because avoiding negative emotions, urges and cravings, and physical sensations that can accompany unpleasant emotions maintains your problem use of alcohol, ERT encourages you to face these experiences as a way to deal with them. The treatment includes two different methods for the direct experiencing of these unpleasant emotions. The first one is called *mindfulness*, in which we will ask you to observe your experience of an unpleasant feeling or sensation with nonjudgmental awareness and without trying to push away or avoid the experience. The goal of mindfulness is to help you "sit with" and not react in the usual way (think alcohol use) to the uncomfortable experience, and to observe how the experience changes with time. We have found that most people report that the unpleasant experience and any accompanying urges or cravings begin to change within minutes of mindfully observing one's mental and physical experience of an unpleasant emotion or uncomfortable physical sensation. This procedure can be quite effective in reducing concerns that the unpleasant experience will only grow more intense and become intolerable. In fact, in most cases, the unpleasant experience is reduced and the individual comes to think about such experiences differently.

The second method of direct experiencing is called *imaginal exposure*, in which we will ask you to experience and recount a high-risk unpleasant emotional drinking situation. The goal of imaginal exposure is to help you process the unpleasant emotional situation by asking you to face the situation during your sessions. We have found that direct experiencing of these unpleasant emotional situations is quite effective in reducing the intensity of the unpleasant emotional response, any related urges or cravings, and physical sensations, and is helpful in increasing a person's confidence in being able to manage future situations without drinking. Also, many people become more aware of the emotions and sensations that have provided the motivation for drinking in the past. Often, this self-knowledge is an important part of the change process for many people who have previously used alcohol to avoid unpleasant experiences. Imaginal exposure can be very effective in reducing the need to "fix" such unpleasant experiences by drinking and engaging in related avoidance behaviors (e.g., having an argument with one's spouse in the kitchen and then leaving the room to go drink in the basement). If you avoid these negative emotional situations by drinking, you do not give yourself the chance to get over your discomfort of these situations without alcohol. This is because until you face these situations, you may continue to believe that they will be intolerable and that your urges and cravings and uncomfortable sensations will remain forever. However, if you face these situations without drinking in a gradual, systematic way, you will find that they can be tolerated and that your emotions and your cravings do not persist indefinitely. Does this idea of directly experiencing emotions make sense to you?

Information Gathering

During this session, your therapist will ask you questions about your history with alcohol and alcohol-related problems, and your current pattern of alcohol use. Your therapist also will want to know what motivated you to seek treatment at this time and any previous treatment that you have received. Finally, your therapist will ask you about your goals for treatment. This is a good time to share other information with your therapist that you believe could be helpful in your treatment.

Emotions and Alcohol

Drinking to manage or regulate emotions is very common. Up to 40% of relapses have been connected with situations that involve unpleasant emotions. At the end of a stressful week, a person may decide to unwind on Friday evening with a few drinks. In order to reduce the aggravation from an unpleasant chore, someone else might have a drink to help get started. Finally, a person may have a few drinks after an emotionally painful event such as a relationship break-up or losing a job. Drinking to manage unpleasant emotions does not automatically mean that a person will develop an AUD. There are many other factors that work together to determine if a person develops an AUD. These factors include whether one or both parents had an alcohol problem, whether they have an anxiety or depressive disorder, the number of close friends who drink heavily, and the number and quality of rewarding activities that are available to them that do not involve alcohol. Usually, it is several factors working together that result in the development of an AUD.

As a person begins to use alcohol more frequently to manage emotions, problems can develop. The amount of alcohol consumed during a drinking episode may increase. As the amount of alcohol and the frequency of alcohol consumption increases, problems begin to occur such as health, social, or legal problems. Sometimes, the negative impact of alcohol use on a person's life is more subtle. A person's thoughts are not as clear and sharp as they used to be or the person no longer feels like pursuing recreational activities or hobbies they used to enjoy. Old friends may "drift" away as the person's alcohol use begins to get in the way of being the kind of worker, parent, or partner they want to be.

During your initial evaluation, you indicated that drinking has caused problems for you and that experiencing uncomfortable or distressing emotions (e.g., anger, irritability, loneliness, anxiety) sometimes leads you to drink. With this treatment, you will learn to regulate your emotions in such a way that you gain more control over them, rather than feeling like you are being controlled *by* them. Therefore, this program will help you better understand the connection between unpleasant emotions and drinking, so that you can learn skills to better manage these emotions when they occur.

Body Scan: Building Physical Awareness

Often, people aren't aware of how or what they're feeling. A person may work for hours and be unaware of the tension in their shoulders; another person may feel "restless" but are not aware of why they are restless. In order to change how we experience and respond to these uncomfortable emotional states, first we have to become aware of them. Now, you might be thinking, "If I become more aware of feeling tense or restless, I'll feel worse! It's better not to think about it." However, just because a person isn't aware of feelings, does not mean it isn't affecting them. Becoming aware of how you feel is the first step to changing how you feel. In fact, not thinking about unpleasant emotions or sensations is a *cognitive* form of avoidance and, as we mentioned earlier, avoidance actually reinforces and maintains the uncomfortable or unpleasant emotions. The same is true for urges and cravings (see the text box).

EMOTIONAL SUPPRESSION VS. ENGAGEMENT

Talking about unpleasant emotions and urges might be considered "off-limits" by some people, and they believe it should be avoided at all costs. Some people deny having urges to drink and may say things like, "I don't think about drinking, I just drink." People who think this way may be engaging in *cognitive avoidance*. That is, they believe that if they admit to having an urge or an unpleasant emotion, then their sobriety could be at risk. They may feel that discussing or drawing attention to urges or emotions may trigger a relapse. Furthermore, they may feel that to admit an urge is to admit that treatment is not working. One example of cognitive avoidance is *suppression*. Suppression is defined as consciously pushing away unpleasant or unwanted thoughts and desires. However, individuals who attempt to suppress urges and unpleasant emotions are more likely to experience "rebound" effects (Sayers & Sayette, 2013). These rebound effects actually make the urges and unpleasant emotions stronger and more frequent. Therefore, it's been suggested that an urge (or unpleasant emotion) should be viewed as a signal alerting the person that something is wrong and requires attention (Bien & Bien, 2002). Both mindfulness and imaginal exposure (i.e., direct experiencing of emotion) promote turning one's attention toward and facing the unpleasant or unwanted experience, rather than pushing it away. When used skillfully, these emotional management techniques allow the person to see that the unpleasant experience will pass. Often, the person gains a deeper understanding of what triggers these emotional experiences and learns to "stay with" or accept the unpleasantness rather than feeling a reactive need to suppress or avoid it. This acceptance of emotions and urges actually helps them pass more quickly, and in the long run, they occur less frequently.

At this point in the session, your therapist will teach you an awareness technique called the *Body Scan*. The purpose of the Body Scan is to increase awareness of physical sensations, which are a component of emotions. Many people also find this activity to be calming. The Body Scan has its origins in mindfulness meditation practice and is used to help develop a person's attention to, and awareness of, physical or bodily sensations. People can have a wide range of physical sensations that they experience, which can include tingling, tightness, pressure, increases or decreases in temperature, or even an itch. You are not searching for anything in particular, just noticing what is there. The goal is simply to become aware of the different areas of your body and allow yourself to experience how each part feels, without trying to change anything. Your therapist will guide you through the exercise. With practice, you can become more open and accepting of uncomfortable physical sensations. Most people find this exercise to be kind of relaxing and interesting, although that is not the primary goal. After you practice the Body Scan exercise, your therapist will discuss your experience with this technique. The best advice we can give you is to be honest. Your therapist will want to know if it felt "weird" or if you found it difficult to keep your attention focused on the task. Believe us, your therapist will have heard those comments—and others—before! The goal is not to experience anything in particular, but simply to experience what is there. No matter how you experienced the brief exercise, you will have been successful in becoming more fully aware of your thoughts, behaviors, and physical sensations in the present moment.

Before you begin the exercise, your therapist will ask you to position yourself comfortably in your chair and close your eyes, if that's comfortable for you. Then you will be guided through the Body Scan exercise. The script is provided next.

Allow your eyes to gently close (or leave them slightly open if that is more comfortable). Place your feet on the floor, and let your body settle, relaxing into the chair, feeling the weight of your body on the chair . . . Take a few slow deep breaths . . .

This Body Scan is about "just noticing" whatever you may be feeling in your body. The goal is not to change anything about what you are feeling, but rather to direct your attention to various parts of the body, becoming aware of any sensations you may be experiencing in the present moment.

Starting with your head, notice any physical sensations you are having in your scalp . . . ears . . . eyes . . . and mouth . . . .

Shifting your attention down now to your jaw . . . throat . . . neck . . . and noticing whatever is there . . . or maybe feeling nothing in particular . . .

Bringing your awareness to your shoulders, and scanning them for any kind of sensations . . . warmth, coolness, tightness . . .

Shifting your attention to your back . . . noting any sensations you are having . . . the pressure of your back against the chair . . . your clothing against your skin.

Some sensations might be pleasant . . . or neutral . . . or unpleasant. Try not label them as good or bad, just notice them, and let them be.

Now tuning in to your stomach . . . your chest . . . aware of how sensations move with the breath, as it comes and goes, following the sensations of your breath, not trying to breathe any certain way . . .

Feeling now your upper arms . . . lower arms . . . and hands . . . becoming aware of any sensations, tingling, tightness, pressure where your arms are resting against something . . .

If you become aware that your mind has drifted to something else . . . this is what minds do . . . just acknowledge where it went, then gently guide your attention back to the body.

Now shifting your attention to your hips . . . thighs . . . knees . . . and noticing whatever is there . . .

Bringing awareness to your lower legs, calves . . . shins . . . feet . . . and toes.

Feeling your feet inside your shoes . . . noticing the bottom of your foot against the sole of the shoe . . . feeling the support of the floor beneath your shoes . . .

Moving back up now, and building an awareness of your body as a whole . . . the legs and hips . . . stomach and chest . . . shoulders, neck, and head.

Noticing your body as a whole . . . its sitting position . . . how that feels . . .

Shifting your attention now to the sounds around you . . .

Noticing any differences between sounds . . .

Gently allow your eyes to open . . .

Your therapist may refer to the Body Scan as "dedicated mindfulness practice." This means that your therapist will talk with you about setting aside or dedicating time each day to practicing this awareness technique. For most people, this should be practiced for at least 5 minutes, twice per day, but you and your therapist will discuss what is best for you.

Stop and Notice: Brief Present-Moment Awareness

A second exercise for building awareness of the present moment is called *Stop and Notice*. As the name suggests, it is intended to be used to just stop and notice what is going on at the moment. This can include becoming aware of what you see and hear around you, and also your own thoughts, emotions, and any urges or cravings for alcohol. As we discussed earlier in this chapter, it is important to become aware of what you are feeling and thinking. This awareness can provide you with important information about the kinds of thoughts, feelings, or situations that contribute to urges and cravings for alcohol, and that could lead to a relapse to drinking. Building this awareness is a first step towards finding more effective ways to manage your emotions and cravings as well as high-risk drinking situations. This technique is brief and can be accomplished almost anywhere during the day. Your therapist will talk with you about using the Stop and Notice technique four times per day.

Identifying High-Risk Drinking Situations via Self-Monitoring

As you begin practicing the Body Scan and Stop and Notice, you will be sharpening your awareness of your present-moment experience. We now want to connect your awareness of the present moment to your use of alcohol. To do this, you will be asked to monitor your urges and cravings to use alcohol and your alcohol use (if you have a drink). We call this *self-monitoring*. If you want to change your drinking, it is helpful to know what comes before and after a drinking episode. You might think that there is nothing that occurs before your alcohol use, or that cravings and urges just appear without any triggering event. Well, if you think about it, something will *always* come before a drink or an urge to drink. Even doing nothing is something; that is, it could be that feeling bored or having nothing to do is what comes before or triggers drinking. In order to become more aware of the things in your life that lead to drinking or an urge to drink, self-monitoring is the most effective tool for understanding your personal drinking triggers. Your therapist will review the self-monitoring log with you and will provide instructions for how to complete it. It is important that you complete the self-monitoring log during the week. Finally, your therapist will ask if you anticipate any high-risk situations during the upcoming week.

Making It Happen

We know, based on years of research, that practicing skills between sessions leads to better treatment outcomes. This is also true for people trying to overcome an AUD. You will be learning skills in this treatment program and you will be asked to practice those skills between sessions. Like learning any new skill, it may seem awkward at first. Also, you will have to remember to practice and to set time aside in your day. As we said in Chapter 2, Practice, Practice, Practice is the key to successful behavior change. Your therapist understands the challenges involved when changing a well-learned behavior like drinking and learning a new behavior to take its place. Having a plan can be helpful. You and your therapist will work on this together at the end of every session. For example, you and your therapist will work collaboratively to modify or adapt the skill practice to fit your schedule and lifestyle. To increase your chance of success, it's important that you develop a plan for skill practice that you feel you can commit to.

Between-Session Skill Practice

☐ **Dedicated Mindfulness** _____

    Body Scan: _____ minutes, _____ times per day

    Making It *Happen*: When and where? _____

    Cues to remember: _____

☐ **Stop and Notice**

    _____ times per day

    Making It *Happen*: When and where? _____

    Cues to remember: _____

☐ **What I hope to gain from treatment:**

    _____

    _____

    _____

☐ **Complete the Daily Monitoring Log.**
☐ **Review the Physical Sensations That Often Accompany Emotions handout and the Emotions List.**
☐ **Bring the workbook to your next session.**

Session Highlights

About Emotions

Emotions serve an important purpose. Emotions help us build closer, more satisfying relationships with others. Emotions get our attention and provide valuable information to help motivate and guide our actions. It's common to think of certain emotions as being "negative"; however, it's their discomfort that makes them so effective in getting our attention and giving us the energy we need to take action. Alcohol interferes with the healthy functions of emotions, stopping them from serving their purpose.

People experience a range of emotions, from pleasant to unpleasant. Emotions are normal and healthy, even those that are unpleasant.

Emotions are like ocean waves that come and go. They rise, getting stronger until they reach the crest, and then subside. They are temporary, so you can ride them out.

In order to manage emotions effectively, you must develop an awareness of them. Emotions include the components of *physical sensations, thoughts,* and *behaviors*. Developing greater awareness of these components will help you identify your emotions. Becoming more aware of emotions is a skill that develops with practice.

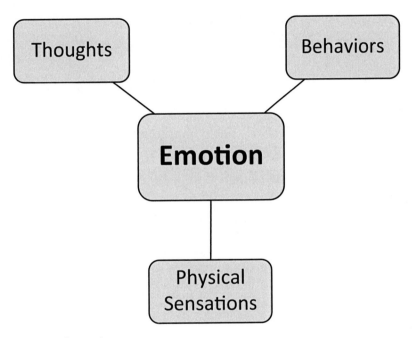

FIGURE 1 Components of Emotion

Emotions and Alcohol

People drink alcohol to regulate their emotions because alcohol can change how they are feeling in that moment. People may drink to make the good times feel even better. Sometimes people drink to manage unpleasant emotions, to "take the edge off" or to numb their emotional discomfort or pain (e.g., anxiety, sadness).

While it may be helpful in the moment, using alcohol to manage emotions can cause problems in the long run. Building skills for effectively managing emotions can help. The goal is for you to be in control of your emotions rather than the emotions controlling you.

Physical Sensations That Often Accompany Emotions

- Various sensations in the chest
- Changes in heartbeat: faster, fluttery, harder (like it will "jump out of your chest")
- Antsy, restless
- Warmth
- Face, ears, neck, or chest flushed and feel hot
- Eyes—hot or stinging, watery (tears)
- Lips, mouth, throat feel dry
- Lump in throat, feels like you can't breathe
- Muscle tightness in various locations such as neck, shoulders, arms, face, mouth, chest
- Clenched jaw, fist
- Feeling cold all over or in hands or feet
- Pain in various areas such as chest, neck, shoulders, stomach
- Appetite changes: either losing or gaining
- Heartburn, upset stomach, nauseated
- "Butterflies" in stomach
- Upset or cramping bowels, gurgling
- Muscle weakness, wobbly knees
- Sweating, all over or just certain places like hands or forehead
- Shaking, quivering, trembling
- Hair standing on end
- Numbness
- Any others not mentioned

Emotions List

General Emotion	Specific Emotions			
	Less		**More**	
Angry	Annoyed Frustrated Irritated Displeased	Hurt Offended Jealous Disapproving	Mad Resentful Furious Enraged Disgusted	Bitter Devastated Contemptuous Hateful
Sad	Down Depressed Lonely	Bored Tired Lazy	Hopeless Empty Despair	Cold Disconnected
Scared	Concerned Cautious Suspicious Vulnerable Worried Nervous	Inadequate Insecure Insignificant Timid Shy	Threatened Shocked Paralyzed Trapped Scared-to-Death	Frightened Abandoned
Guilty	Embarrassed		Ashamed Shameful	Humiliated
Helpless	Hesitant Unsure Insecure		Pressured Overworked Overwhelmed	Exhausted Depleted
Confused	Curious Bewildered	Skeptical Suspicious	Numb Disoriented	
Confident	Competent Energetic Respected Responsive	Appreciated Optimistic Hopeful	Discerning Successful Valued Nurtured Worthwhile	Proud Noble Triumphant Daring
Grateful	Appreciative	Kind	Delighted	Indebted
Secure	Calm Relaxed Open	Quiet Thoughtful Humble	Loved Safe Peaceful Protected	Warmth Understood Accepted
Happy	Playful Creative Sensuous Cheerful Content	Enthusiastic Optimistic Accepting Expectant	Hopeful Stimulated Imaginative Alive Joyful	Jubilant Ecstatic Talkative Nurturing

Daily Monitoring Log

Situation Who, Where, When, What	Emotion Rate Intensity From 1 to 100	Thoughts	Physical Sensations What Did you Notice?	Desire to Drink Thought, Craving, or Urge 1 to 100	Actions
By myself, at home, evening . . .	Bored—50	I just want to drink; one might be okay.	Antsy, restless	70	Rode bike, listened to music

Day, date	Mon, 3/25					
Number of standard drinks	0					
Skill Practice	✔					

Chapter 4

Session 2

Enhancing Motivation and Mindfulness

Session 2 Goals

- Identify the benefits and costs of drinking.
- Learn about your high-risk drinking situations.
- Learn about mindfulness, and continue developing present-moment awareness of thoughts, emotions, and physical sensations.
- Learn a second technique for developing present-moment awareness.

Overview

In Session 2, you and your therapist will take a few minutes to review your goals for treatment and your therapist will explain how this treatment can help you achieve your goals. You will discuss the benefits and costs of drinking and clarify your reasons for wanting to change your drinking at this time. Also, you will begin to identify situations that pose a risk to your sobriety and learn how to use the self-monitoring record from Session 1 to examine your thoughts, feelings, and physical sensations in these situations and how they contribute to your alcohol use. Next, you will learn more about mindfulness and how it can be used to increase your awareness of the present moment. In ERT, mindfulness is used to increase your awareness and acceptance of emotions, urges and cravings, and accompanying physical sensations. Mindfulness compliments the identification of high-risk situations by increasing your awareness of external events (e.g., too many demands made upon you, a conflict with someone, being on vacation, a holiday party), as well as internal reactions (e.g., irritated, on edge, wound up, pounding heart, muscle tension) that trigger your drinking. Finally, you will learn a mindfulness technique called *Object-Centered Mindfulness*. The goal is to strengthen your mind's capacity to sustain your attention to the present moment.

Weighing the Benefits and Costs of Drinking

When faced with making a change in some aspect of their behavior, most people weigh the benefits and costs of the various options or alternatives available to them. Your decision to receive treatment for an alcohol problem may have both benefits and costs. The benefits may be that your relationships will improve, and that you will experience fewer alcohol-related work and health problems, among others. The costs of entering treatment may be the money, time, and effort required to successfully change your drinking behavior. Because you are reading this workbook, it is likely that the scale tipped in favor of the benefits of changing your drinking.

For some people, however, it's not that straightforward. Although they have sought out treatment, they may be unsure about changing their drinking. These people are not convinced that the benefits of change outweigh the costs. Conducting a decisional balance exercise is a way to clarify a person's reasons for changing and not changing. As you are completing the decisional balance exercise that follows, be as honest as you can. List as many benefits and costs you can think of that are personally relevant to your decision for wanting to change your drinking. Your therapist will review and discuss your responses with you when you are finished. Following the treatment session, you can continue to add additional benefits and cost of continuing to drink versus changing your drinking.

Weighing the Benefits and Costs of Drinking

Example

CONTINUE TO DRINK AS BEFORE

BENEFITS	COSTS
Helps me relax	*Hurts my relationship*
Enjoy being with drinking friends	*Bad for my health*
	Costs me jobs
	Can't get things done

ABSTAIN FROM ALCOHOL

BENEFITS	COSTS
Better marriage	*I'll miss the feeling*
Feel better physically	*How to deal with my feelings*
Feel better about myself	
Get things done	

Worksheet

CONTINUE TO DRINK AS BEFORE

BENEFITS	COSTS
_____	_____
_____	_____
_____	_____
_____	_____
_____	_____

ABSTAIN FROM ALCOHOL

BENEFITS	COSTS
_____	_____
_____	_____
_____	_____
_____	_____
_____	_____

More About Mindfulness

At this point in the session, your therapist will review the concept of mindfulness with you and how we use it in ERT as a means for increasing your ability to observe, identify, and manage unpleasant thoughts, emotions, and physical sensations. The term *mindfulness* is an English translation of the Pali word *sati*, which also means *awareness, attention,* and *memory*. Although mindfulness is rooted in the ancient religion and philosophy of Buddhism, you do not have to believe in Buddhist principles or become a student of Buddhism to develop mindfulness. Mindfulness, as used in this treatment, is not associated with any religion. In fact, mindfulness is a simple form of awareness that is available to everyone at any moment. Mindfulness involves paying attention in a particular way, on purpose, in the present moment, with a mindset of mild curiosity or interest. Mindfulness has been used for many years to help people manage stress, regulate emotions, cope with chronic pain, and improve other aspects of mental and physical health. You will use mindfulness to increase your awareness of any thoughts, emotions, or physical sensations associated with an urge to drink alcohol. A mindful approach may be used directly to help manage urges and cravings. In the next session, you will be introduced to a technique called *Watch the Wave* (also known as *Urge Surfing*), which is a skillful way to cope with urges or cravings that involves observing them without giving in to them. Next, we discuss two more mindfulness exercises: Mindful Observing and Object-Centered Mindfulness.

Mindful Observing

During the last session, you learned a mindfulness technique called *Stop and Notice* in which you were asked to Stop and Notice what was taking place in the present moment. If you extend this present-moment awareness a bit more, this allows you to take the next step and engage in Mindful Observing or Watching. This brief mindfulness exercise provides an opportunity to put some distance between the "observer" and what is being observed in the moment, which could be an emotion, thought, urge to drink, or something going on in the environment. It's as if the observer climbs out of the river onto the riverbank, sits down, and begins observing what is going on. This "observing" is done with an attitude of mild curiosity, without getting caught up in the intensity of the experience. Being less caught up in the intensity of an experience can help people to make decisions about what to do next, decisions that are different than the unhealthy decisions they may have been making. One of the advantages of Mindful Observing is that it can be used nearly anytime, anywhere.

In-Session Skill Practice: Object-Centered Mindfulness

The Stop and Notice and Body Scan exercises that you learned during Session 1 are types of mindful activities. With the first mindfulness exercise, you had to Stop and Notice what was taking place in the present moment. With the Body Scan, you were asked to become aware of physical sensations. Today we introduced Mindful Observing. You will learn a second mindful activity today that is called *Object-Centered Mindfulness*. The name is pretty self-explanatory. Your therapist will have you select one object from among several different objects available and will instruct you to focus your attention on only that one object. You will use primarily your sense of touch and sight as you bring your attention to rest on the object. At this point you may be asking, "What does this have to do with my drinking?" We understand how you may have that question. To answer this question, it is useful to remember that your mind (that is, your attention) can wander. For example, if you're working on a complex and somewhat frustrating problem at work, it is possible that your mind may wander to thinking about the first drink you will have after the workday ends. In that moment, your attention is no longer directed to the present moment that involves the frustrating problem, but it is directed forward in time. That's right, urges and cravings can be thought of as future-oriented (e.g., "I look forward to having that first drink."). In fact, it is likely that your mind is very good at wandering; most people's minds are that way. It's what our minds do. By focusing on a single object, that is, practicing mindfulness, you can strengthen the ability of your mind to remain with any mental task or object in a sustained way. Your ability to focus your attention on present-moment awareness will be important to gaining a deeper understanding of the cognitive, emotional, and physical sensations that can activate your desire to drink. As you become better at observing and describing your experience, you will be in a better position to change your reactions to high-risk drinking situations.

For the Object-Centered Mindfulness exercise, you will select one item from the variety of objects that your therapist will show you. Choose one object to focus on and, without touching it, begin looking at the object with mindful awareness.

Take a few slow deep breaths, bring yourself to the present moment . . .
 Take a few moments to really look at this object. Look at it as if you have never seen one of these before, like this is the first time . . .

What do you notice about it? . . .

What do you notice when you look at the surface? . . . Is it smooth? . . . bumpy? . . . rough? . . .

What about its shape? . . . Its edges? . . .

Are there any shadows? . . . Where are they? . . .

What do the edges of the shadows look like? . . . Are they clear and distinct, fuzzy or blurred? . . .

Move your head slightly so different parts of it come into view. What do you notice? . . . Observing any changes . . .

Now reach out and touch it. What do you notice? . . . Do you feel the pressure on your fingers? . . . Move your fingers over the surface. What does it feel like? . . .

Pick it up with your fingers? . . . Turn it over (or around), and look at it from different angles, watching the details shift . . . Notice how it feels where it comes in contact with your skin . . .

Slowly place it into the palm of your hand, feeling its weight . . . What else do you notice? . . .

Slightly move your hand, watching what happens . . . Does the object move? . . . How does it feel against your skin as your hand moves? . . .

Softly close your hand around it, and slowly drop your hand, until it is resting comfortably.

Gently allow your eyes to close . . . and bring your attention to the sense of the body breathing . . . each breath coming and going as it will, not having to breathe any certain way . . . (about 10 seconds)

Allow your attention to expand beyond the breath to the entire body . . . with a sense of curiosity . . . noticing any sensations in the body . . . . . . (about 10 seconds)

Shift your attention now to sounds . . . not trying to listen, but just noticing whatever sounds come into your awareness . . . . . . (about 10 seconds)

Gently allow your eyes to open . . .

Making It Happen

As we said before, Practice, Practice, Practice is the key to successful behavior change. Your therapist understands the challenges involved when changing a well-learned behavior like drinking and learning a new behavior to take its place. In this session, you evaluated the pros and cons of behavior change. Thinking about the positive consequences of changing your drinking may help motivate you to practice the skills between sessions.

Between-Session Skill Practice

☐ **Dedicated Mindfulness**

Object-Centered Mindfulness: _____ minutes, _____ times per day

Making It *Happen*: When and where? _____

Cues to remember: _____

☐ **Mindful Observing**

_____ times per day

Making It *Happen*: When and where? _____

Cues to remember: _____

☐ **Optional—Add additional costs and benefits to Weighing the Benefits and Costs of Drinking worksheet.**
☐ **Complete the Daily Monitoring Log.**
☐ **Bring the workbook to your next session.**

Session Highlights

Mindfulness is paying attention in a particular way, on purpose, in the present moment, with a mindset of mild curiosity or interest. Mindfulness has been used for many years to help people manage stress, regulate emotions, cope with chronic pain, and improve other aspects of physical and mental health.

When being mindful, you can direct your attention toward one thing, like an object, or the sensations of the breath. You can also broaden your attention to include noticing whatever it is you are experiencing in the present moment such as sights, sounds, physical sensations, emotions, thoughts, or urges to act.

Mindful Observing

When your intention is to keep attending to your experiences in the present moment, even for just a minute or two, that's a kind of mindfulness known as *observing*. It's as if you are watching your moment-to-moment experiences without getting caught up in them.

Observing brings about a "pause" and creates a space in which you can change your course of action rather than continuing your old, unwanted behaviors on autopilot.

Think of it this way: If going through your usual day-to-day routine on autopilot is like being carried along by the current in a river, going wherever the current takes you, then being mindful is making a choice to get out of the river and climb onto the riverbank. You are no longer going wherever the current takes you. Instead, you have pulled yourself out. Now you have a chance to see where you are, to observe the river's current rather than being carried away by it, and to choose your direction instead of it being chosen for you.

A Note About Wandering Minds

Sometimes people think they won't be able to use the skill of observing because their minds wander too much. It's true that minds wander and it's expected that your mind will wander, too! The goal here is *not* to "try really hard" to pay attention. Instead, whenever the mind wanders, briefly acknowledge where it went, and gently bring it back to the present moment. Realizing your mind has wandered and bringing it back is normal and not a sign that you are unable to observe your moment-to-moment experiences. In fact, you will have just observed your mind wandering!

FIGURE 2 **Minds wander; it's what they do.**

Daily Monitoring Log

Day & Date	Situation *Who, Where, When, What*	Emotion *Rate Intensity 1 to 100*	Thoughts *What thoughts were you having?*	Physical Sensations *What did you notice?*	Desire to Drink *Thought, Craving, Urge 1 to 100*	# of Drinks	Behaviors *What did you do? What skills did you use?*
mon 3/25	By myself, at home, evening	Bored 50	I just want to drink one might be ok.	Antsy, restless	70	3	Body Scan, rode bike, listened to music.

Chapter 5

Session 3

High-Risk Situations and Mindful Coping

Session 3 Goals

- Identify personal high-risk situations for drinking.
- Learn about the use of alcohol for avoiding unpleasant emotion and craving.
- Learn several mindful coping strategies for managing emotions and craving.

Overview

In this session, you and your therapist will discuss the topic of high-risk drinking situations. A high-risk situation can be any situation that increases the likelihood of drinking for you. You and your therapist will spend time working together to identify your unique high-risk drinking situations. Next, you will discuss the topic of alcohol cravings, also referred to as urges. Your therapist will talk with you about your experience with urges and cravings, and how you cope with or manage them. Finally, you will be introduced to the following mindful coping skills: (1) Watch the Wave (also known as *Urge Surfing*), (2) Mindful Breathing, and (3) Mindful Moments. These skills can be used to manage both emotions and urges and cravings.

High-Risk Situations

Because high-risk situations differ from person to person, you will begin to identify those situations that pose an increased likelihood of drinking for you. It's important to note that a high-risk situation does not have to be a specific event or place; it could be a certain time of the day, or a long stretch of time with no personal obligations or responsibilities. They are alike in that they all increase the likelihood of drinking. Being with certain people may also increase your risk for drinking. You will use the High-Risk Situations and Coping Plans worksheet found in this chapter to write down some of your high-risk situations. Don't be too concerned if you can't think of any on the spot; some common categories of high-risk situations have been included in the following box to get you thinking about the people, places, and things in your life that increase the likelihood of drinking for you. Your therapist will also be asking you some guiding questions to help you think about the kinds of situations that would pose a challenge to your sobriety. Once you know more about these situations, you can begin to learn ways to help you manage these situations without drinking.

COMMON HIGH-RISK SITUATIONS

- Seeing alcohol or other people drinking.
- People, places, times of day, and situations commonly associated with drinking (such as drinking buddies, parties and bars, getting home from work, weekends).
- Emotions (such as frustration, fatigue, feeling stressed out). Even positive emotions (elation, excitement, feelings of accomplishment) can prompt a desire to drink.
- Thoughts, such as how good you imagine it would feel to use alcohol, that you can have "just one" without a problem, that you deserve a reward, want to get away from it all, or need a drink to handle a problem.

Alcohol, Unpleasant Emotions, and Craving: The Problem With Avoidance

It's common for people with AUD to manage their unpleasant emotions, physical sensations, or urges and cravings by drinking. The problem is that each time you drink and your emotions and cravings decrease, the habit of avoiding these unpleasant experiences by drinking gets stronger (see Figure 3). Although it is common for people to want to escape or avoid experiencing unpleasant emotions and sensations, the problem is that avoiding discomfort may make you feel better in the short run, but in the long run avoidance can prolong your recovery from AUD. However, as your therapist will show you, if you *stay with* the unpleasant emotions, sensations,

Uncomfortable → *Drink* → *Relief from* → **MORE LIKELY TO**
emotion   *alcohol*   *uncomfortable emotion*   **DRINK NEXT TIME**

FIGURE 3

and cravings long enough, they will decrease. In this treatment, you and your therapist will spend a good deal of time focusing on uncomfortable emotions, physical sensations, and urges or cravings related to your alcohol use. Importantly, you will learn strategies that can help you increase your ability to tolerate the uncomfortable sensations and help you feel more in control of your ability to manage them effectively without drinking. Of course, we do not suggest that you place yourself in high-risk drinking situations. However, there are some things you cannot avoid, like unpleasant emotions. They are a natural part of everyone's life. One goal of this treatment is to help you learn to accept, tolerate, and find alternative ways to manage uncomfortable experiences without the use of alcohol.

Urges and Cravings

Urges and cravings are common and natural reactions to addictive behaviors. Their presence does not mean that you are weak or have a character flaw. For people trying to abstain from alcohol, urges and cravings are often experienced as uncomfortable or unpleasant. These types of urges and cravings have been called *abstinence urges* (Tiffany, 1990) and are often experienced by people receiving treatment for an AUD. Although urges and cravings are unpleasant, it's important not to give in to them. When giving in to them by drinking, for example, the behavior of drinking is strengthened via the process of negative reinforcement, or the removal or reduction of the unpleasant feelings and sensations. Although urges can be difficult to tolerate, over time urges actually decrease in intensity. It helps to think of urges and cravings as temporary, or as ocean waves that rise up, crest, and then subside. In this way, it becomes possible to imagine yourself as a surfer who patiently rides out the wave. Urges typically last only a few minutes and rarely more than 10 minutes. Most people, however, tend to give in to their urges before they get to experience the decrease in intensity. For people with an AUD, "giving in" to urges usually means drinking or making the decision to drink when alcohol becomes available (see Figure 4).

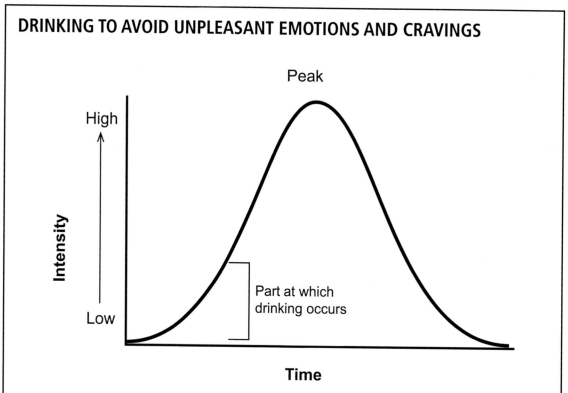

FIGURE 4 Emotion and Craving Wave Over Time

Figure 4 illustrates the time course of an unpleasant emotion (or craving). Notice how drinking occurs at a lower level of emotional intensity and well in advance of the peak or highest level of discomfort. By drinking early on in the development of the unpleasant emotional response, the person avoids experiencing more intense levels of negative emotion.

In this session, you will learn an emotion regulation technique that we call *Watch the Wave*. It can be applied to both unpleasant emotions and cravings because both function like waves that increase, peak, and subside. Watch the Wave is adapted from a popular technique called *Urge Surfing*, developed by Marlatt and Gordon (1985). It's a method of coping with urges that has been used successfully for quite some time. You will identify one or more situations that trigger your cravings and urges. The idea behind Urge Surfing is to become mindfully aware of the craving or urge without giving in to it. For example, instead of acting on your urges and cravings in your usual way, your therapist will guide you in paying close attention to the various thoughts, feelings, and sensations that arise as the urge unfolds. With practice, you learn to skillfully observe your direct experience in the moment. You will begin to deepen your awareness of any physical sensations or discomfort that come before your use of alcohol. Instead of fighting against your urges or giving in to them, you can learn to accept them and ride them out. The idea is not to make the craving or urge go away, but to experience it in a different way. Remember, when urges and cravings are pushed away or suppressed, they tend to get stronger. With Urge Surfing, you "step aside" and Watch the Wave as it comes and goes, with a mindset of interest or mild curiosity. With practice, you can become like the skilled surfer who rides the wave until it crests, breaks, and subsides.

Emotion Regulation Skills

In this section, your therapist will introduce you to several emotion regulation skills. All of the skills can be used to help you develop emotional awareness. The more aware you are of your emotions, the more flexibility you will have in how you choose to respond to them. The first three are mindful coping skills and the last one, Name the Emotion, is designed to help you build your emotion vocabulary.

Watch the Wave

In Session 2, you were introduced to the idea of "watching" or observing what you are experiencing from moment to moment. In addition, you participated in an in-session exercise called *Object-Centered Mindfulness.* In that exercise, your attention was focused on an external object. You can also observe or watch your internal experiences such as physical sensations, thoughts, and emotions. This too is a mindfulness skill, just watching or observing whatever you are experiencing in the moment. Being an observer means that you have taken a step back from what is happening in the moment. Observing in the moment with this little bit of space is different than suppressing or pushing away uncomfortable feelings or thoughts. They are still there, but they just don't seem as powerful or overwhelming as they did before. When you apply this skill to your emotions, you are no longer trying to push them away or suppress them. Instead you note their presence and watch as they come and go from the perspective of an observer, having put a little space between you and what you are observing within yourself.

Remember that emotions and urges are like waves. They're always changing. As you observe or watch them change, you will see how they start small, reach a peak, and then subside. As you Watch the Wave, you will begin to see that craving, urges and emotions are not permanent. You may begin to feel like you no longer need to react to them by drinking.

Mindful Breathing

When you are being mindful, you are deliberately paying attention to what is happening in the present moment. As you develop this skill, you become increasingly aware of your thoughts, emotions, physical sensations, cravings, and urges as they occur, and can ride them out as they come and go. You no longer have to react automatically in the same old way every time your buttons get pushed. Instead, this kind of awareness gives you more control over your actions, and that includes drinking. Your therapist will teach you another skill that you can use to manage or cope with uncomfortable feelings and sensations. It's called *Mindful Breathing*. You don't have to breathe in a certain way; you just notice your breath as it comes and goes.

With Mindful Breathing, you remain in the present moment, using your breath as an anchor. You can practice Mindful Breathing at times when you are calm or when any uncomfortable thoughts, sensations, or emotions enter into your field of awareness. At those times, keep breathing and "just notice" the uncomfortable sensations with a mindset of mild interest or curiosity, not judgment. Just "breathe with them and through them," neither pushing them away or clinging to them. Like the choppy surface of the ocean, the mind can become agitated in response to a challenging situation. Below the surface, however, there is only a gentle swell (see Figure 5). As you learn to focus on your breath, you remain calmer and gain more control over your actions.

Your therapist will lead you through a Mindful Breathing exercise. You will be seated comfortably in your chair, and your therapist will ask you to focus on the sensations of your breath as it comes and goes. Allow your breath to come and go without interfering or attempting to control it. Mindful Breathing is about strengthening your attention and awareness, not controlling your breath. The script is provided next.

Begin by getting comfortable. Place both feet flat on the floor. Do something comfortable with your hands. Sit with your back, neck, and head in alignment. Sit in a way that promotes alertness and wakefulness. Let your eyes close gently. Notice your feet on the floor, your back against the chair, your hands resting where they are, and your face and head where they are. Allow yourself to feel the heaviness of your body. Allow yourself to relax into the support of the chair and the floor beneath you. Let your body ease and settle as much as possible.

Bring attention to your stomach. Allow it to relax and become soft. Let it stay soft. Focus on the sensation of your breath as it comes and goes. Focus your attention at the place in your own body where you can feel your breath come and go most easily and naturally. For some this is the abdomen, for others the chest, and for others the nose or even the mouth (if you tend to breathe with your mouth open). Let your attention settle and focus exactly on that place where the breath sensations are easiest for you to feel. If you aren't sure exactly where to focus, the abdomen is a good place to start. Let your attention rest there now. Allow yourself to feel the sensation of the breath moving in and out of the body just as it is.

Allow the breath to come and go without interfering or trying to control it. This practice is about strengthening your attention and awareness, not controlling the breath. Keep the focus on just this breath. Let go of any thoughts about how many breaths or the next breath or the last breath. Just this breath. If it helps you to focus, you could whisper quietly to yourself "in" on the in breath, "out" on the out breath, and "pause" or "space" for the space between the breaths. Try to remain present for the entire cycle of each breath: in, out, pause, in, out, and so on. As your attention strengthens and mindfulness grows, you can begin to notice the beginning of the "in" breath, the middle, and the end. You can do the same for the "out" breath.

Let your attention settle more deeply into the variety of sensations of the breath in the body. Allow the feeling of the rise and fall of the abdominal wall, the actual stretching sensation, to be the focus. Notice the changing patterns of sensation, how each breath is different—some shallow, some deep, some strong, some weak, some choppy, some smooth. Meet each breath as if sensing it for the first time. In truth, each breath is here once and only once. Welcome it.

When your attention wanders away from the breath, gently notice where it went. It could be a thought, or a sound outside. No matter where your mind wanders, with patience and kindness, bring your attention gently back to the place in the body where you are concentrating on your breathing. Praise yourself for noticing that your attention has wandered. This is what minds do. Recognizing when the mind wanders is a moment of mindfulness. It is a part of becoming more present in the moment.

As you continue to focus on your breathing, keep your belly soft. Notice if there is tightening and tension in the body. Allow softening and relaxing as much as possible. Keep practicing this way for a few more minutes. If you notice feelings such as restlessness, boredom, fear, anxiety, or sleepiness building and demanding your attention, gently notice that. Notice any tendency to fight them. Try to let them be and return your attention to your breathing. Okay, you can open your eyes now and stretch if you like. Notice how you feel, and then let that feeling go.

Mindful Moments

The final mindful coping skill that your therapist will review in this session is something we call *Mindful Moments*. This is something that you can easily do every day, multiple times per day. It's about quieting your mind, and becoming aware of what you are feeling and more intentional in your actions. It's about being fully present in whatever you are doing in the moment. You can be mindful while engaging in most any activity. This includes eating, walking, showering, washing dishes, or gardening, to name a few. Simply focus your attention on just this one activity. Use your sense of touch, smell, taste, sight, and sound to become more aware in the present moment. Remember, Mindful Moments are intended to be brief, so 1 or 2 minutes each time you practice is sufficient. Of course, you can always extend the time, if you like.

FIGURE 5 Find Calm Below the Surface with Mindful Breathing

Name the Emotion

Although we can't always choose what emotions to feel or when to feel them, developing emotional awareness will provide you with greater flexibility in how you choose to respond to what you are feeling. Many people have found the **Emotion List**, located in Chapter 3, to be very useful throughout treatment as they build a working vocabulary of words to describe their emotions. At any time during your day, consult the **Emotion List** to find the emotion word that best captures what you are feeling in the moment. You may want to mark that page with a sticky note or some other method for quick reference. You may also want to find out if other emotion lists are helpful. Many therapists have developed helpful emotion word lists. An Internet search can also produce lists of emotion vocabulary words.

Making It Happen

As you continue to identify your high-risk drinking situations, write them down. Then, for each situation, identify an alternative behavior that you will do instead. Ideally, the alternative behavior will be one of the skills that you are learning in this treatment program. For example, if coming home after work is a high-risk drinking situation for you, ask yourself what you can do instead. Can you imagine your urge or craving as an ocean wave that rises up, crests, and then subsides? Can you engage in 3 to 5 minutes of Mindful Breathing? As you're driving home from work, it may help to visualize yourself engaging in the alternative behavior. Keep it simple. Focus less on the outcome and more on implementing the alternative behavior that can lead to the outcome you desire.

Between-Session Skill Practice

☐ **Dedicated Mindfulness**

Mindful Breathing ＿＿＿＿＿ minutes, ＿＿＿＿＿ times per day

Making It *Happen*: When and where? ＿＿＿＿＿＿＿＿＿＿＿＿＿＿＿＿＿＿

Cues to remember: ＿＿＿＿＿＿＿＿＿＿＿＿＿＿＿＿＿＿＿＿＿＿＿＿＿＿

☐ **Mindful Moments**

During: ＿＿＿＿＿＿＿＿＿＿＿＿＿＿＿＿＿ , ＿＿＿＿＿ times per day

Making It *Happen*: When and where? ＿＿＿＿＿＿＿＿＿＿＿＿＿＿＿＿＿

Cues to remember: ＿＿＿＿＿＿＿＿＿＿＿＿＿＿＿＿＿＿＿＿＿＿＿＿＿＿

☐ **Complete the Daily Monitoring Log.**
☐ **Watch the Wave when you experience an urge or craving to drink.**
☐ **Name the emotion at least one time per day.**
☐ **Continue adding high-risk situations to the High-risk Situations and Coping Plan worksheet.**
☐ **Bring the workbook to your next session.**

Session Highlights

We know that alcohol cravings and emotions come and go, like waves, and that both emotions and cravings can be uncomfortable.

People may try to push the urge to drink and uncomfortable emotions away, but trying to suppress them isn't always effective. Sometimes they return, even stronger than they were before. In addition to being ineffective, continuing to suppress, escape, or avoid discomfort by using alcohol reinforces or strengthens the drinking behavior, making it increasingly difficult to stop drinking.

Effectively Managing Discomfort

Instead of avoiding or suppressing discomfort, consider allowing yourself to experience and ride out the wave of temporary discomfort that comes along with unpleasant emotions and cravings or urges to drink in a way that's manageable, using the following skills.

1. Watch the Wave

Whether you are experiencing emotional discomfort or an urge or craving to drink, observe or Watch the Wave, noticing with a nonjudgmental mindset of gentle interest whatever it is you are experiencing such as physical sensations, emotions, thoughts, or urges to act. As you watch, stay with your present-moment experiences, and ride out the discomfort as it comes to a peak and then subsides. You may breathe mindfully as you Watch the Wave.

2. Breathe Mindfully

You can help yourself feel more "settled" when you want to manage or cope with discomfort by bringing your attention to your breathing. Like the choppy surface of the ocean, we can become agitated in reaction to a difficult situation. Below the ocean surface, there is only gentle swelling. As we focus on our breathing "below the surface," we remain calmer and have more control over our actions. See Figure 6 below.

3. Mindful Moments

As you are going about your day, use your different senses to become more aware in the present moment. Simply focus your attention on just one activity. Use your senses (touch, smell, taste, sight, and sound) to become more aware in the present moment.

4. Name the Emotion

Simply naming your emotion (e.g., "I am feeling frustrated.") can help you regulate the emotion. In the case of unpleasant emotions, Naming the Emotion can make the experience of the emotion less intense. By reducing the emotions intensity, you are then better able to respond more effectively.

FIGURE 6 Find Calm Below the Surface With Mindful Breathing

High-Risk Situations and Coping Plan

List your potential high-risk situations on the left and coping strategies on the right. As you progress through treatment, return to this plan to add additional high-risk situations and newly learned coping skills.

High-Risk Situations   Coping Strategies

1. _____   _____

    _____   _____

                                           _____

2. _____   _____

    _____   _____

                                           _____

3. _____   _____

    _____   _____

                                           _____

4. _____   _____

    _____   _____

                                           _____

5. _____   _____

    _____   _____

                                           _____

6. _____   _____

    _____   _____

                                           _____

Daily Monitoring Log

Day & Date	Situation *Who, Where, When, What*	Emotion *Rate Intensity 1 to 100*	Thoughts *What thoughts were you having?*	Physical Sensations *What did you notice?*	Desire to Drink *Thought, Craving, Urge 1 to 100*	# of Drinks	Behaviors *What did you do? What skills did you use?*

Chapter 6

Session 4

Drinking-Related Thoughts, Coping With Urges and Cravings, and Cognitive Reappraisal

---

Session 4 Goals

- Review between-session activities and skill practice.
- Learn about drinking-related thoughts.
- Learn coping skills for managing thoughts, urges, and craving to drink.
- Learn how thoughts influence our emotions and behaviors.
- Learn how to manage emotions and cravings with a skill called *Cognitive Reappraisal*.

Overview

In this session, you and your therapist will discuss the influence of thoughts on emotions and behavior. You will first review some common thoughts that people have about alcohol that can lead to drinking. Thoughts about drinking are normal and you and your therapist will spend some time talking about the types of thoughts that you have had regarding alcohol and alcohol use. As you develop greater awareness of your drinking-related thoughts, you can then begin to question or challenge the accuracy of those thoughts that in the past have increased your risk for drinking. By changing how you respond to your thoughts, you create an opportunity to gain more control over your drinking behavior. Remember, the goal is not to keep you from having thoughts about drinking; it's to keep you from *acting* on those thoughts.

Also, you will take a closer look at how your thoughts can influence your emotions; that is, how you think about situations and events has an impact on your emotions in a situation. You and your therapist will discuss an effective method for managing emotion-generating thoughts that is called *Cognitive Reappraisal*. Reappraisal involves changing the meaning of a situation so that the emotional response to the situation is also changed. When you do this, the emotions you experience lose a bit of their intensity and this can free up some mental energy that will allow you to better manage the situation that triggered the emotions. Your therapist will ask you to identify your own thoughts that affect your emotions, and will then work with you to develop one or more different ways to think about (or reappraise) the situation. By thinking differently about the situation, we mean thinking about the situation in a way that changes your emotional response to the situation, which, in turn, can decrease your risk for drinking.

Finally, as we have said before, there are a number of similarities between craving and emotions. You will learn how you can use Cognitive Reappraisal to regulate your craving for alcohol.

Drinking-Related Thoughts and Coping Skills

Your therapist will direct you to the information sheet titled "Thoughts That May Lead to Drinking," which you can find at the end of this chapter. You will spend this part of the session identifying and talking with your therapist about the types of drinking-related thoughts that you experience most often. Your therapist will ask you which thoughts about alcohol seem to be the most common and in which situations those thoughts are most likely to occur. Next, your therapist will review with you eight coping skills and strategies for managing your thoughts. These skills are also useful for managing urges and cravings to drink and may be added to the "Coping Strategies" column on the High-Risk Situations and Coping Plan worksheet you began in Session 3. The goal here is to make you aware of your thoughts and to provide you with some skills for managing thoughts that can help to keep you on track with your sobriety.

Cognitive Reappraisal: Managing Emotions

Imagine this situation: You have been abstinent for a month and are being invited to a party by an acquaintance from work. You recently began working together on a long-term project and you accept the invitation because you feel it would be good for your work relationship. Because it's a co-worker's party, you assume there will be others at the party whom you know and can socialize with. When you arrive, you don't recognize anyone. After the host introduces you to a few other guests, within minutes you find yourself standing alone in the crowded space. You feel self-conscious just standing there and you can feel yourself getting more and more uncomfortable. You have always experienced some mild social anxiety when meeting new people, but you could tolerate the uncomfortable feelings when you were drinking. After one or two drinks, you also found it easier to talk to people. However, because you are no longer drinking, you find it more difficult to join a conversation. As you stand there, you think to yourself, "I must look really weird standing here with no one to talk to. Everyone else is talking with someone. What's wrong with me?" These thoughts begin to add to your distress. You begin to feel warm and you notice that your heart is beating faster. As your mouth gets dry and you begin to perspire slightly, you wonder if other people notice what is happening and are thinking that you are strange and don't fit in with other people at the party. You think to yourself, "After I say hello, I won't know what to say next. There is going to be this uncomfortable silence and the other person will think I'm kind of weird and uninteresting."

In this situation, you can see how the thoughts are creating an emotional downward spiral. How could you think differently about this situation to turn this around? Could you have prepared in advance for this situation? Are your thoughts about the situation accurate? How might someone else view this situation? You and your therapist will take a closer look at these questions and come up with some alternative ways of thinking about the situation that could help reduce the emotional intensity of the situation. For example, by reappraising the situation in a less negative way, your emotional intensity would be reduced, which can increase your chances of making this a more enjoyable evening.

Once you become aware of how your thoughts are ruling your emotions, you can begin to reframe the situation using the following three steps.

1. **Breathe.** Stop and take a few slow breaths. This will disrupt the problematic thought process and produce a calmer state.
2. **Identify.** Identify the thought that is causing you the most distress. For example, "People will think I'm uninteresting and will want to get away from me."
3. **Reappraise.** Finally, try to reappraise your thoughts about the situation to change the type of thought you are having, which is likely to also change the intensity of your emotional response. Just the *act* of engaging in Cognitive Reappraisal can

make the situation less distressing. For example, "I can't know what a person is thinking," or "I am an interesting person; they just don't know me well."

Of course, as we've said from the beginning, learning any new skill takes some practice. You may not succeed the first time, but it's important to keep trying. Next, you and your therapist will apply this same method of Cognitive Reappraisal to a personally relevant situation. Ideally, the situation is one that could lead to an increased risk for drinking.

In the example we have been discussing, you can see that by engaging in a Cognitive Reappraisal of the situation, the level of unpleasant emotion decreased. Cognitive

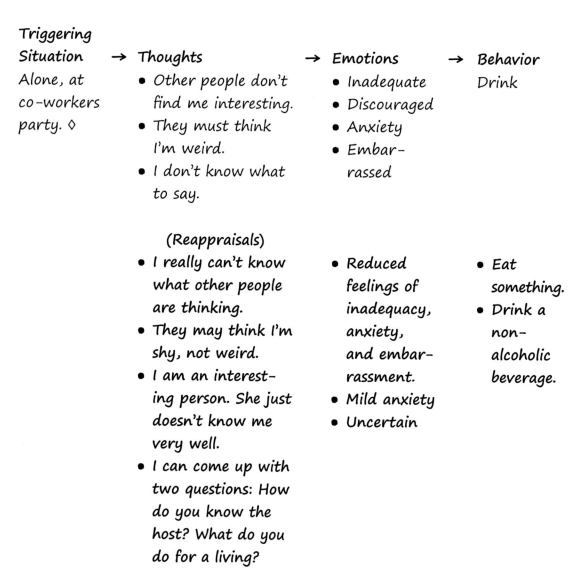

Triggering Situation	→	Thoughts	→	Emotions	→	Behavior
Alone, at co-workers party. ◊		• Other people don't find me interesting. • They must think I'm weird. • I don't know what to say.		• Inadequate • Discouraged • Anxiety • Embarrassed		Drink
		(Reappraisals) • I really can't know what other people are thinking. • They may think I'm shy, not weird. • I am an interesting person. She just doesn't know me very well. • I can come up with two questions: How do you know the host? What do you do for a living?		• Reduced feelings of inadequacy, anxiety, and embarrassment. • Mild anxiety • Uncertain		• Eat something. • Drink a non-alcoholic beverage.

FIGURE 7 Using Cognitive Reappraisal to Manage Emotions

Reappraisal can be applied to many unpleasant emotional drinking situations to help manage the emotions that can trigger the urge to drink.

When it comes to managing your emotions, it's important to slow down and become aware of your thoughts and emotions. Using your mindfulness skills, observe your thoughts and emotions in the situation. Let them come and go. When you're ready, follow the three-step outline shown earlier to help you regulate your emotional response to challenging situations.

In-Session Skill Practice: Cognitive Reappraisal

The following exercise corresponds to the Thought Reappraisal worksheets located at the end of this chapter. Working with your therapist, you will apply the skill of Cognitive Reappraisal to a personally relevant unpleasant emotional drinking situation. Use one of the two Managing Emotions: Thought Reappraisal worksheets provided at the end of this chapter to generate several Cognitive Reappraisals. Pay particular attention to your emotions before and after the reappraisal. Discuss with your therapist the changes in emotion and behavior that would result from conducting a reappraisal of the identified situation.

Cognitive Reappraisal: Managing Urges and Cravings

There are a lot of similarities between cravings and other emotional responses. Like emotions, urges and cravings can be regulated using Cognitive Reappraisal. Reappraising your desire for alcohol or thinking about alcohol in a different way can be very effective in decreasing your alcohol cravings. Your therapist will talk with you about an effective strategy that you can use to reduce your desire to drink. The strategy involves either focusing on the negative consequences of drinking alcohol (e.g., negative impact on health, puts a strain on important relationships, hangover, lost productivity) or focusing on the positive consequences of not drinking (e.g., I will feel good about myself, I will have more energy tomorrow, more likely to stay married). To help you identify a personal list of both negative and positive consequences of drinking or not drinking, you and your therapist will review the decisional balance exercise that you completed in Session 2.

Early in treatment, when people are choosing to abstain from drinking, craving is often experienced as unpleasant or uncomfortable. It's common for people to have thoughts such as "I can't tolerate this" or "I don't know how I'm going to get through the day without drinking." Thinking this way can bring about feelings of hopelessness or despair. Cognitive Reappraisal can be used to regulate your emotions that result from the experience of craving. For example, one way to reappraise your experience of craving as intolerable would be as follows: "While it's uncomfortable right now, I know that the craving will eventually pass." Or, "If I wait a few minutes, the discomfort will be gone."

At the end of this chapter you will find a Managing Urges and Cravings: Thought Reappraisal worksheet. Use this worksheet to generate several Cognitive Reappraisals for thoughts related to the discomfort of experiencing an urge or craving alcohol.

Making It Happen

By now you know some of the challenges involved when changing a well-learned behavior. If you are finding it difficult to complete the between-session skills practice, talk to your therapist. Sometimes, certain thoughts or beliefs about treatment such as, "I shouldn't have to work so hard in treatment," may be getting in the way of making a commitment to practicing skills. By talking with your therapist you may find an alternative way to view your treatment experience. For example, "Learning any new behavior requires some effort, but it's worth it if I can achieve my goal." Remember, your thoughts can derail the best laid plans. By becoming aware of your thoughts you can identify those that may be undermining your skill practice.

Between-Session Skill Practice

☐ **Dedicated Mindfulness**

   (Your choice) _____ , _____ minutes, _____ times per day

   Making It *Happen*: When and where? _____

   Cues to remember: _____

☐ **Mindful Moments**

   During: _____ , _____ times per day

   Making It *Happen*: When and where? _____

   Cues to remember: _____

□ **Identify any drinking-related thoughts. Write them on the Daily Monitoring Log.**

□ **Use coping skills and strategies reviewed in this session for managing your urges and cravings. Add these skills to the High-risk Situations and Coping Plan worksheet.**

□ **Complete the Thought Reappraisal worksheet.**

□ **Complete the Daily Monitoring Log.**

□ **Bring the workbook to your next session.**

Session Highlights

Thoughts are constantly going through our mind. How we think affects how we feel, which in turn, influences our actions or behaviors (see Figure 8).

Increasing our awareness and evaluating what is going through our minds can help us manage our emotions. As a result, we are better able to actively choose our actions or behaviors, including those related to drinking.

One way to manage thoughts that negatively affect our emotions and behaviors is through a process known as *Cognitive Reappraisal*. Simply put, reappraisal means thinking about your situation differently or viewing it from a different perspective.

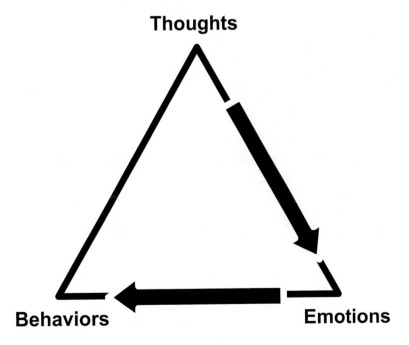

FIGURE 8 Relationship of Thoughts to Emotion and Behavior

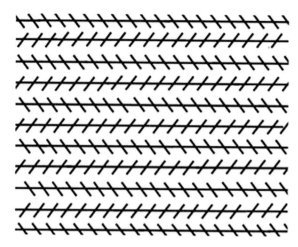

FIGURE 9 Things Are Not Always as They First Appear

Sometimes our minds can play tricks on us (see Figure 9). For example, the lines above may look wavy, but if you look more closely they are actually parallel. Things seem to be a certain way, when they are not. By thinking about our situation differently, we may find that our perspective broadens such that emotions and behaviors become more manageable.

Once you become aware of how your thoughts are ruling your emotions, you can begin to reframe the situation using the following three steps.

1. **Breathe.** Stop and take a few slow breaths. This will disrupt the problematic thought process and produce a calmer state.
2. **Identify.** Identify the thoughts that are causing you the most distress.
3. **Reappraise.** Finally, try to reappraise your thoughts about the situation to change the type of thought you are having, which is likely to also change the intensity of your emotional response. Just the *act* of engaging in Cognitive Reappraisal can make the situation less distressing.

   - Is there another way think about this situation?
   - How might others think about this situation? (What would I say to someone else in this situation?)
   - Are my thoughts and interpretations accurate?
   - What could I learn from this situation?
   - Might there be some positives here I haven't considered?
   - Is this thought "just a thought"?

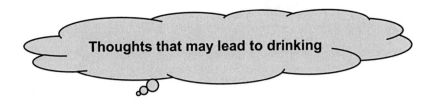

Thoughts that may lead to drinking

☐ **Nostalgia**—Fondly remembering the "good old days" when you drank; usually the parts that weren't associated with any problems or consequences of drinking. Fantasizing about drinking in the future including only the short-term positive effects.

☐ **Testing control or curiosity**—"I bet I can have just one without a problem." "What would it be like to have just one?" "Let's see if I can leave a six-pack for guests."

☐ **Crisis**—"I need a few drinks to handle this one." "I went through so much, I deserve a drink."

☐ **Feeling uncomfortable when sober**—"Now that I don't drink, I'm short-tempered. Maybe it's better to be good-natured than to stop drinking right now."

☐ **Self-doubts**—You doubt your ability to control your desire or drinking behavior. "I just have no willpower." Or, "I've tried to quit before and it didn't work. Why should this time be any different?"

☐ **Escape**—"I just want to get away from it all." To get away from problems, discomfort from unpleasant situations, conflicts, memories, thoughts, unpleasant emotions, boredom/restlessness, sleeplessness, or low self-image.

☐ **Relaxation**—"I just want to unwind—right now" (without having to do anything else to relax).

☐ **Socialization**—"I just need a drink to feel more at ease, more talkative, less awkward . . ."

☐ **To hell with it**—"Why bother trying? Nothing really matters!"

☐ **Other**—_____

_____

_____

_____

Coping With Thoughts, Cravings, and Urges

The desire to drink can come in the form of thoughts, cravings, and urges to drink. It can range from very mild to very strong.

Thoughts, Cravings, and Urges to Drink

- May be uncomfortable but are common and normal, and don't mean something is wrong.
- Occur more often earlier in treatment. The desire to drink lessens and gets easier to manage as abstinence continues.
- Are time limited. They come and go, and will pass with time.
- Are weakened when you get through them without drinking. Each time you let them pass without drinking, your ability to manage them effectively is strengthened.

Coping Skills	
✓ **Avoid, leave, or change the situation.** Try a different activity; avoid people and places associated with drinking; remove alcohol from the house.	✓ **Self-reinforcement.** Remind yourself of your successes so far. For example, usual drinking situations in which you have remained abstinent, using new skills, and other successes.
✓ **Challenge the drinking thoughts.** Identify the drinking thought and then challenge it.	✓ **Decision delay.** Put off the decision to drink for 15 minutes while the thought, craving, or urge passes.
✓ **Remember why.** Remember the benefits of not drinking and the negative consequences of drinking.	✓ **Talk it through.** Talking about the desire to drink or the reason behind it (like stress) can be very effective.
✓ **Eat a good meal or snack,** have a nonalcoholic drink, or have something very sweet.	✓ **Distract yourself** with other thoughts. Think about something pleasant, and unrelated to drinking.

Thought Reappraisal

Example 1: Daughter's Wedding

Before Reappraisal

<u>Thoughts</u>

- I'm going to have a hard time talking to people, no alcohol to help me loosen up and socialize.
- Everyone's going to notice I'm not drinking . . . they'll think it's weird.
- I feel like such a loser.

<u>Emotions</u>

- Nervous, anxious
- Embarrassed
- Inadequate

<u>Behaviors</u>

- Skip the reception, think of excuses not to go.
- Give up and have a drink just this once.

After Reappraisal

- This is my first time doing this without alcohol. I'll never have to do it for the first time again.
- Some might notice, but they might be more curious than anything else.
- (For "I feel like such a loser"), A thought is just a thought.

- Still nervous, but also a little hopeful (it'll get easier).
- Embarrassed, but not as much.
- Not inadequate . . . maybe uncertain?

- Easier to abstain.
- Think of ways to make myself feel more comfortable when I'm there.
- Make some specific plans to keep from drinking.

Example 2: A Stressful Day at Work

Before Reappraisal

<u>Thoughts</u>
- What a terrible day!
- They don't know how much I have to do every day.
- They don't appreciate me.

<u>Emotions</u>
- Aggravated
- Overwhelmed
- Unappreciated

<u>Behaviors</u>
- Snap at people.
- Drag my heels.
- Be unproductive.
- Drink or think about drinking.

After Reappraisal

- Well, it's over now and I got through it. I've had worse.
- Maybe they actually didn't realize how much I already had to do or how long it takes.
- Come to think of it, they did say how much they appreciated my help.

- A bit more confident (I can get through tough days).
- Not aggravated . . . Maybe just annoyed.
- Pleased.

- Easier to abstain
- Tell people I had a rough day.
- Decide to take it easy tonight, put my feet up.
- Have some good food.
- Go to bed earlier than usual.

Managing Emotions: Thought Reappraisal Worksheet

High-Risk Situation _____

Before Reappraisal

Thoughts	Emotions	Behaviors

After Reappraisal

Thoughts	Emotions	Behaviors

Managing Emotions: Thought Reappraisal Worksheet

High-Risk Situation _____

Before Reappraisal

Thoughts	Emotions	Behaviors

After Reappraisal

Thoughts	Emotions	Behaviors

Managing Urges and Cravings: Thought Reappraisal Worksheet

High-Risk Situation _____

Before Reappraisal

Thoughts	Emotions	Behaviors

After Reappraisal

Thoughts	Emotions	Behaviors

Daily Monitoring Log

Day & Date	Situation *Who, Where, When, What*	Emotion *Rate Intensity 1 to 100*	Thoughts *What thoughts were you having?*	Physical Sensations *What did you notice?*	Desire to Drink *Thought, Craving, Urge 1 to 100*	# of Drinks	Behaviors *What did you do? What skills did you use?*

Chapter 7

Session 5

Drink Refusal Skills and Managing Emotions With Actions

Session 5 Goals

- Review between-session activities and skill practice.
- Learn the two types of "social pressure" situations that can increase risk for drinking.
- Identify your social pressure situations.
- Develop a personalized plan for resisting pressure to drink.
- Learn a strategy for managing your emotions with actions.

Overview

Now that you have made a commitment to changing your drinking, "social pressure" from friends or others can make it difficult for you to stick to your goals. In the first part of this session, you and your therapist will discuss two types of social pressure situations that can increase your risk for drinking—direct and indirect. You will identify the social pressure situations that you are most likely to come across and then discuss strategies for how you can handle these situations.

In the second part of this session, your therapist will share with you a method for managing your emotions that involves changing your *behavior*. Changing the way you act or respond to your emotions can have the following benefits:

- Increase your ability to tolerate or accept the physical feelings that go along with strong emotions

- Reduce the intensity of unpleasant emotions
- Reduce the need to engage in a behavior such as alcohol use when experiencing unpleasant emotions
- Increase self-confidence for managing unpleasant emotions

Each emotion has its own set of behaviors. By definition, emotions are associated with urges to act in particular ways. For example, fear creates the urge to escape, sadness creates the urge to withdraw, and anger creates the urge to fight. Of course, people do not always act on these urges. Although these actions may have been adaptive for our ancestors, in today's world some urges to act may be ineffective, unhealthy, and even harmful to that person. For example, if you are upset with your boss, picking an argument with her or him may lead you to lose your job. One way to manage emotions is to take a different action or to substitute an adaptive behavior for an unhealthy behavior. A common strategy involves choosing an alternative action or "acting the opposite" to what the emotion is "urging" or motivating you to do (Barlow, Allen, & Choate, 2004; Linehan, 1993, 2015).

Drink Refusal

Rationale for Drink Refusal Skills

Drink refusal skills address two forms of social pressure that are often experienced by individuals in recovery: direct and indirect social pressure. Direct social pressure occurs when someone directly offers you a drink. This is most likely to happen in high-risk drinking situations such as get-togethers, weddings, backyard barbeques, and other celebratory social events. Indirect social pressure occurs when a person returns to the same old places (e.g., bars, restaurants, parties), with the same people, doing the same things, and experiencing the same feelings previously associated with drinking. With indirect social pressure, no one directly offers you a drink. Rather, you feel tempted to drink just by being around others who are drinking. In this type of situation, you may feel "deprived" or "left out," or you may remember the positive consequences of drinking such as enhancing pleasure or that socializing was more fun when drinking. While you may not drink when around others, you may begin having thoughts about leaving and returning home and having a drink.

Direct Social Pressure

As you and your therapist begin looking at direct social pressure, the therapist may begin by asking you to think about some situations where you experience this type of pressure to drink. Although it's helpful, especially in the early stage of abstinence, to avoid people, places, and things that are drinking-related (e.g., bars), everyone will eventually encounter a situation in which they will experience social pressure to drink. Being offered or pressured to drink is a very common high-risk situation for individuals who have decided to stop drinking. Your therapist will ask you a few questions about what it's like to feel pressure to drink.

- *Have you received such offers?*
- *Do you have someone in your life who offers you drinks or pressures you?*
- *What is that like for you?*

Indirect Social Pressure

As you remain abstinent, you will likely encounter situations in which you are in the company of other people who are drinking. Although no one has directly offered you a drink, just being around others who are drinking can be tempting. Because other people around you are drinking, it can begin to feel that drinking might be okay. Your therapist will begin this part of the session by asking you about your experiences with indirect social pressure across these and other situations.

Sometimes it can be difficult to identify examples of indirect social pressure. You might remember feeling tempted in situations where others were drinking, but blamed this temptation on internal factors such as your cravings or thoughts about drinking (i.e., remembering the short-term positive effects of alcohol). To help you better understand indirect social pressure, your therapist will provide several examples that do not involve alcohol. For example:

> *Imagine your son or daughter playing Little League baseball. It is picture day and the parents are given large white envelopes and asked to select the photo package they wish to purchase. You don't want to purchase the photos but you look around and see that every other child's parent is holding an envelope and people are putting checks into the envelopes. Do you purchase a photo package or not?*
>
> *A co-worker asks for a donation to a charitable organization and you do not want to contribute, but everyone else in the room begins pulling out money. What do you do?*

Some examples of indirect social pressure situations that involve alcohol include:

- Locating your assigned table at a wedding reception and noticing that the champagne glasses have already been filled and people are raising their glass for a toast.
- Being invited to a sporting event and sitting in a private box where the alcohol is free and everyone is drinking.
- Attending a business meeting and the waiter is pouring everyone a glass of wine and asks you if you prefer red or white.
- You arrive at a friend's summer barbeque and there are tubs filled with ice-cold beer. Everyone seems to have a beer in their hand.

After discussing your experiences with direct and indirect social pressure situations your therapist will summarize what they have learned from you.

Next, you and your therapist will discuss the reason for rehearsing drink refusal skills.

Rationale for Rehearsing Drink Refusal Skills

1. The risk for a lapse or relapse may be greater if a person does not have adequate drink refusal skills.
2. Drink refusal requires an assertive response that involves more than just a sincere desire to stop drinking.
3. The use of alcohol in social gatherings is very common.
4. Skill rehearsal increases the strength of the connection between the situation and your behavior; that is, you will be prepared to respond quickly and efficiently in social pressure situations.

When therapists introduce the topic of drink refusal skills, some people feel like these skills don't apply to them. They often will say that they have no problem turning down a drink or saying "no" to someone who offers them a drink. Tell your therapist if you feel this way. Drink refusal skills can be a bit more complicated than just saying no and your therapist can help you decide how to make the most of this session's content. For example, if you feel well-prepared to manage direct social pressure situations, you may decide to spend more time discussing indirect social pressure situations. Your therapist may also discuss some situations that you haven't considered before. For example, you may feel like you have no problem turning down a drink from your friends and family, but how about your boss or a client whose business you are trying to attract?

Regardless of your skill level, how you choose to respond to an invitation to drink will vary, depending on who is offering the drink and how the offer is made. Sometimes, a simple "No, thank you" will be enough. At other times, additional strategies will be necessary. In some cases, you may choose to tell the other person about your prior drinking problem as this may be useful in eliciting helpful support; at other times, it will be unnecessary to share that information. In this session, you and your therapist will explore the many varieties of drink refusal skills and discuss how these skills can be tailored to your life and experiences.

Next, you and your therapist will work together to develop a plan for coping with both direct and indirect social pressure situations. Using the Drink Refusal Skill Practice worksheet at the end of this chapter, you will list your social pressure situations and then discuss some ways to cope with the situations. Your therapist will begin by asking you about your preferred coping strategy and will review the pros and cons of using a specific strategy in a given situation.

With any social pressure situation, your goal is to learn to say "no" quickly and in a convincing manner. The more you rehearse your response to these situations, the more likely it is that you will have your response at the "tip of your tongue." To get you started thinking about drink refusal skills, a typical plan is provided for you here:

- Get a nonalcoholic drink ahead of time.
- Plan an exit strategy from the situation *before* you enter it.
- Say "no" first.
- Suggest something else to eat, drink, or do:
  "No thanks. Would you like to take a walk instead?"
  "No thanks, but I'd sure like a cup of coffee."
- Ask the person to stop offering you a drink.
  "No thanks, no need to keep offering. I'll let you know if I change my mind."
- After saying "no," change the subject.
- Use your body language:
- Use a clear, firm, unhesitating voice.
- Make direct eye contact.
- There's no need to make excuses or feel guilty:
  You have the right *not* to drink!

IN-SESSION EXERCISE: DRINK REFUSAL SKILLS

You will have time to practice new drink refusal skills in session. You will be asked to identify a specific situation in which you experience social pressure to drink. Your therapist will want to know why this situation is difficult for you. Your answers to these questions will help create a role-play situation that is directly applicable to your life. A few examples of questions your therapist might ask are:

- *Tell me the "where, when and who" of a situation where someone frequently or strongly pressures you to drink.*
- *What would they say or how would the person say it?*
- *So they wouldn't take "no" for an answer. What would the person say next?*

Once you and your therapist have gathered important details of the situation, you will engage in a few role plays. While some people feel uncomfortable at the idea of a role play, we observe that generally, clients find the role plays quite useful. For example, you can find and practice the words that are most comfortable for you, which will make it easier to respond the next time that you encounter this type of situation. For the first role play, you will play yourself and your therapist will play the part of the person who is offering you a drink. This will provide your therapist the opportunity to directly observe your drink refusal skills.

Following the role play, your therapist will ask you a few questions about your experience. For example:

- *Great! What do you think you did well?*
- *What do you think you could improve on next time?*
- *How did it feel?*
- *Any situations coming up for you where you anticipate being pressured to drink?*

Often, your therapist will offer some constructive feedback, review other options available to you in that situation, and, if time permits, will practice the skills one more time.

Managing Emotions With Actions

You have already learned how avoiding unpleasant emotions only serves to prolong them. If you use alcohol to manage or reduce unpleasant emotions, physical sensations, or cravings, it's likely that these unpleasant experiences and your use of alcohol will continue. In ERT, the goal is to learn how to manage these unpleasant emotions and physical sensations without drinking. In this part of the session, your therapist will introduce a way to manage your unpleasant emotions with actions. Managing or changing emotional responses often involves a behavioral strategy we refer to as "acting the opposite"; that is, acting in a way that is inconsistent with the emotion (Barlow et al., 2004; Linehan, 1993, 2015). To understand how you can modify your emotions with actions, take a moment and review Figure 10.

Figure 10 illustrates the reciprocal relationship between thoughts, emotions, and behaviors. At the base of the triangle you can see that the relationship between behaviors and emotions is a two-way street. That is to say, your emotions can influence your behavior *and* your behavior can influence your emotions. In ERT, the primary goal is to learn how to manage your unpleasant emotions without drinking. In Session 4, you learned how to change your emotional response by changing your thoughts. In this session, you will learn how to change your emotional response by changing your behavior. Learning these skills provides you with options in managing your unpleasant emotions.

Before coming to treatment, you may have drank alcohol (a behavior) to help manage an unpleasant emotion. But how do you manage this unpleasant emotion when you are no longer drinking? What action can you take to help you manage this emotion? Consider the following example:

Suzy is feeling sad and depressed and these feelings encourage her to withdraw from social contact and drink. While these actions have brought about some short-term relief from her sadness and depression in the past, any benefits she feels are temporary. In the long

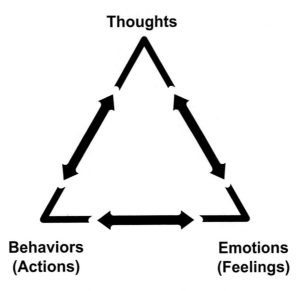

FIGURE 10 Relationship Between Thoughts, Emotions, and Behaviors

run, Suzy recognizes that isolating herself from other people and drinking has made her unhappiness worse. In addition, she recognizes that her lack of activity and her drinking are unhealthy. However, she is at a loss for what she can do to change how she feels.

In this example, Suzy's actions are to withdraw and drink. What would an alternative action be? Well, she could call a friend and go for coffee or take a walk. Instead of staying home and climbing under the covers, she could engage in a productive activity like shoveling the neighbor's sidewalk or ironing her clothes for the week. There are any number of alternative actions that Suzy could choose from. The important point, however, is that by taking action Suzy is engaged in activities that could increase the chance of positive interactions with another person, improve her health, or provide her with a feeling of accomplishment. By taking action—an action that is inconsistent with the urge to withdraw and isolate herself—Suzy's emotions may change or become less intense. It's a way of changing her emotions by changing her behavior. How might her emotions change? A few examples are provided here:

- She increases the possibility of a positive social encounter (e.g., friend shows interest, smiles, compliments her).
- She feels productive.
- Feels good about herself for helping out another person.
- Increased activity reduces her worries about her health.

By engaging in an alternative action, or one that was opposite to the emotion-driven urge to withdraw, Suzy has used her behavior to change or modify her emotions.

In-Session Skill Practice: Managing Emotions With Actions

Using the Managing Emotions With Actions: Skills Practice worksheet located at the end of this chapter, your therapist will ask you to identify a recent situation in which you experienced an unpleasant emotion and the action that the emotion was urging you to take. You will write this down on the top panel of the worksheet. Next, working collaboratively with your therapist, decide on an alternative action in response to the emotion. Usually, the alternative action is opposite to the action the emotion is urging you to take. So, for example, if you were angry at your boss and the anger was prompting you to yell or walk out of work, an alternative action might be to breathe calmly, soothe yourself, and then approach your boss at a later time when your anger had subsided and you had a chance to think about what you would like to say. Write the alternative action in the bottom panel of the worksheet and also write down how taking this alternative action would make you feel. To further guide you as you learn to manage emotions with actions, here are some helpful steps to remember.

Steps for Managing Emotions With Actions

1 **Stop and Notice**
   - Use this mindfulness skill to increase awareness of unpleasant emotions and urges to act. Cue or prompt yourself to Stop and Notice several times each day by setting an alarm on your phone or posting a note that you see throughout the day.
2 **Identify the Emotion**
   - If necessary, use the Emotions List from Session 1 in this workbook.
   - Use your thoughts and physical sensations to guide you.
   - Ask yourself if this is an emotion that you want to change.
3 **Evaluate the Urge to Act**
   - What does this emotion make me feel like doing?
   - Is this a good idea?
   - Is it helpful?
   - Is it healthy?
   - Will it help me achieve my goals?
   - Will it keep me safe?
   - Will it keep me sober?

Note: If the specific action you have the urge to take would be helpful or a good idea for the situation and it fits with your goals of a healthy behavior that avoids drinking, then give yourself the "go-ahead" to take the action. However, if the specific action you have the urge to take would not be healthy or helpful, or does not fit with your goals of health and abstinence, then choose an alternative action. This is a way of behaving or "acting" yourself into feeling differently.

4 Choose an Alternative Action
- A guideline is to consider actions that are in some way opposite or inconsistent with your initial urge to act.
- Remind yourself of your goal, which is to regulate or change the emotion.
- You can ask yourself, "What healthy or helpful action will help me achieve my goal?"
- Let's brainstorm some ideas.
- What is the first step? The second step?

5 Take Action
- Take a deep breath and take action!
- Re-evaluate your emotion.
- Give yourself a big pat on the back for facing a challenging situation.

When to Act on Your Emotions

There are times when it may be necessary for you to respond to the urge to act on an emotion. If the actions that go along with the emotion are helpful and keep you safe, then you can take action. For example, if you find that you are in an unsafe situation, go ahead and follow your urges to take actions that will help you stay safe. Another example involves being overcharged by your cable or telephone carrier for the second time. In this situation, your anger may be justified. If you were angry and you did *not* express your anger, the problem may remain unresolved, it could be repeated on your next monthly bill, and your anger would be prolonged. In this case, it would be acceptable to express your anger in an *effective* way. An ineffective expression of anger such as yelling at or threatening someone could end up hurting you in the long run (i.e., other person hangs up leaving your problem unresolved and creating more problems for you).

Making It Happen

When learning any new behavior, it is helpful to practice in an environment that is relatively free from distraction. Be creative! The only quiet place may be your car as you're driving to and from work. Others may find peace while taking a shower or when weeding the garden. The point is to make it a bit easier on yourself when first learning the skills.

Between-Session Skill Practice: Drink Refusal Skills

☐ **Dedicated Mindfulness**

(Your choice) _____ , _____ minutes, _____ times per day

Making It *Happen*: When and where? _____

Cues to remember: _____

☐ **Mindful Moments**

During: _____ , _____ times per day

Making It *Happen*: When and where? _____

Cues to remember: _____

☐ **Complete Drink Refusal Skill practice.**
☐ **Choose an emotion to regulate/manage with actions, and complete the Managing Emotions With Actions Skill Practice worksheet.**
☐ **Complete the Daily Monitoring Log.**
☐ **Bring the workbook to your next session.**

Session Highlights

Social Pressure

Social pressure to drink may be direct or indirect. Both types can pose a threat to your sobriety. Direct pressure involves someone offering you a drink or exerting pressure on you to have a drink. Indirect pressure involves being tempted to drink by being around others who are drinking—even though you have not been directly offered a drink. Resisting social pressure to drink can be difficult. Why? Some reasons include fear of rejection by others, wanting to avoid ridicule, not wanting to hurt someone's feelings, or being uncertain about what you really want. Take time to recognize your social pressure situations and review the drink refusal skills covered in this session. Remember, you have the right to choose your own path.

Managing Emotions With Actions

Emotions influence our actions (e.g., we feel afraid and we run, hide, or stand and fight) and our actions influence our emotions (e.g., drinking alcohol to reduce anxiety or sadness). Because drinking is not a healthy option for you, alternative actions must be identified to help manage your emotions. In the case of unpleasant emotions, you must ask "What does this emotion make me feel like doing?" If the answer involves an unhealthy or not very helpful action, then choose an alternative action. A common strategy involves "acting the opposite" to what the emotion is "urging" or motivating you to do. For example, if you are feeling shame you may have the urge to hide your behavior from others or avoid others you may have harmed. Acting opposite, in this example, would be to disclose your behavior to someone who would not reject you (e.g., an AA sponsor, a therapist, a close and trusted friend).

Steps for Managing Emotions with Actions

1. Stop and Notice
2. Identify the emotion
3. Evaluate the urge to act
4. Choose an alternative action
5. Take action (remembering that sometimes the best action may be *no* action)

Drink Refusal Skill Practice

List below people who might offer you a drink in the future. Take a moment to think about how you will respond to them and write down your responses.

People who might
offer you a drink

Drink refusal response

_____ _____

_____

_____ _____

_____

_____ _____

_____

_____ _____

_____

In-Session Skill Practice: Managing Emotions With Actions

Situation _____

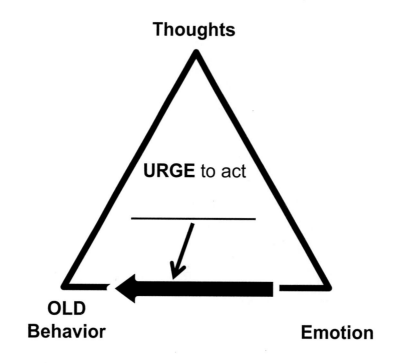

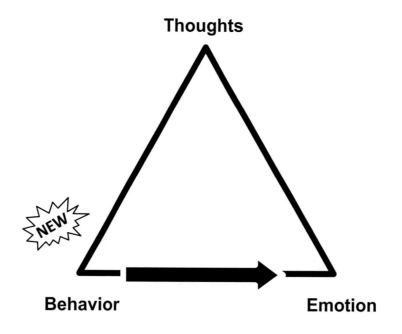

Between-Session Skill Practice: Managing Emotions With Actions

Situation _____

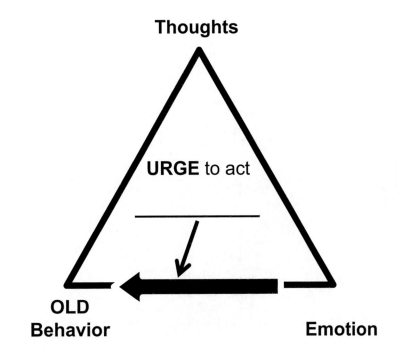

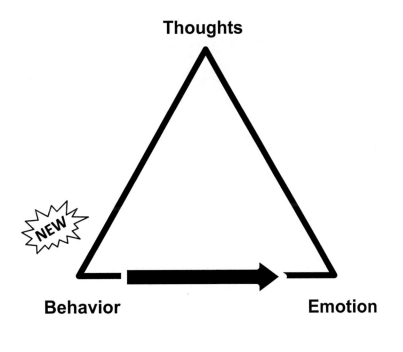

Daily Monitoring Log

Day & Date	Situation Who, Where, When, What	Emotion Rate Intensity 1 to 100	Thoughts What thoughts were you having?	Physical Sensations What did you notice?	Desire to Drink Thought, Craving, Urge 1 to 100	# of Drinks	Behaviors What did you do? What skills did you use?

Chapter 8

Session 6

Skill and Treatment Progress Review and Preparing for Direct Experiencing of Emotion

---

Session 6 Goals

- Review the skills learned up to this point.
- Evaluate progress towards treatment goals.
- Prepare for direct experiencing of emotion using guided imagery.

Overview

Your therapist will review with you all of the CBT and ERT skills that you have learned thus far in treatment. Your therapist will ask you which skills you use most often and those you find most useful. Of course, whether or not a skill is useful will depend on the situation and at what point during the situation you are using the skill. For example, Cognitive Reappraisal may be more useful before you enter a situation and less useful when you are actually in the situation and your emotions are at a high level.

Your therapist will then take you through a guided imagery exercise to familiarize you with using imagery to practice managing emotions that are related to your desire to drink. You'll also identify and gather information about your specific situations that involve uncomfortable emotions which increase your risk for drinking.

This chapter contains additional information about problem-solving skills that you may explore on your own. As you abstain from drinking, certain problems may improve on their own without additional effort on your part (e.g., more money to pay bills, fewer days absent from work). However, day-to-day problems will continue to arise and you will need a way to approach solving these problems so that they don't build up and place you at increased risk for relapse. The problem-solving method outlined in this chapter can be used to address many types of problems.

It may also be used in combination with your ERT skills to solve problems that produce unpleasant emotions.

Review of Treatment Goals and Progress

This is the midpoint of the treatment program. Your therapist will check in with you regarding your drinking goal and progress toward that goal.

When you entered treatment, your drinking goal was _____
_____.

How would you rate your progress towards this goal? _____
_____.

If you haven't achieved your goal, what do you think would help you reach your goal?
_____
_____

What is your goal at this time? _____
_____

Whether you have made progress toward your goal, but still have some work to do, or you've met your goal and you want to maintain it, the midpoint of treatment is a good time to review the skills covered thus far to see which ones have been working for you.

Skills Review

By this point in treatment, we hope that you understand how the skills you are learning can help you manage unpleasant emotions, thoughts, and sensations that are related to your use of alcohol. We hope that you are spending time each day practicing these skills, to help you with regulating your emotions. You should be practicing mindfulness every day, and if you're not, then you should be identifying with your therapist barriers to practice so that you can get back on track. In addition to your mindfulness skills practice, we know that having a broad range of skills that are used consistently and flexibly are associated with better alcohol treatment outcomes. Are you using only one skill? Or are you using different skills in different situations? Finally, within any given situation, are you able to switch to using a second skill if the first skill doesn't seem to be working? Some challenging situations may require drawing upon multiple strategies or types of strategies, and adjusting your approach throughout the situation (e.g., discontinue one strategy and choose another).

We know that practicing skills requires effort but we also know that the more you practice, the less effort it takes to complete the skill practice. The more time you can give to planning and practicing skills, the more benefit you will get out of it. In this part of the session, you and your therapist will be reviewing the skills you've learned since the beginning of treatment. Using the Menu of Coping Skills and Strategies at the end of this chapter will help you develop your personalized "skills toolbox" that you can use for selecting the right skills for each type of situation; that is, it will help you "choose the right tool for the job." The overall goal is to improve your ability to respond skillfully to a wide range of challenging situations that are high risk for drinking.

The Menu of Coping Skills and Strategies lists all of the skills covered in treatment thus far. As you review the list, your therapist will ask you which skills you have found most helpful and if you have any comments or questions. The skills to be reviewed are:

- Mindful Observing
- Stop and Notice
- Body Scan
- Object-Centered Mindfulness
- Self-monitoring
- Watch the Wave (also called *Urge Surfing*)
- Other coping skills for managing urges and cravings (i.e., avoid people or situations, decision delay, food or nonalcoholic drink, talk to a friend, distraction)
- Mindful Breathing
- Cognitive Reappraisal
- Drink refusal skills
- Managing emotions with actions

Your therapist will respond to any questions and will encourage you to "try the skills out" whenever possible. Mindfulness skills can be practiced almost anytime, anywhere. Other skills such as Cognitive Reappraisal and drink refusal skills may be used to prepare for upcoming high-risk situations. Finally, some skills will be used in the moment, and when you are actually experiencing a craving or emotional response. Skills to use in these situations are Watch the Wave and Managing Emotions With Actions.

Problem Solving

We continually are faced with difficult or challenging situations. In order to function effectively, we must find ways to solve the day-to-day problems we face. Excessive or uncontrolled drinking is a problem and seeking treatment is one approach that a person can take to resolve the problem. However, even as you reduce your problem use of alcohol, difficult and challenging situations will continue to emerge. If you don't have a good way to address these problems, they can build up over time and the negative consequences that result from unresolved problems (e.g., anxiety, depression, relationship problems) can increase your risk for relapse. Therefore, a problem-solving approach can be a useful means of dealing with life's many difficult and challenging situations. After reviewing the skills you have learned up to this point in treatment, you are ready to use a problem-solving method to: (1) generate a variety of possible solutions to the problem, and (2) increase the chances that you will select the most effective response from the possible solutions that you generated to solve the problem. By learning problem solving, you will be learning a skill that can be used to cope effectively in a wide range of situations.

Problem-Solving Exercise

Use the Problem Solving worksheet in this chapter to write down your responses when working each of the steps described in this section. To begin the problem-solving exercise, think of a current problem you encounter that you would like to solve. Ideally, the problem is one that you currently face on a regular basis (e.g., at least weekly). Choosing a problem that you are currently facing will provide you with the opportunity to try out the problem-solving approach, determine if the approach works well, and make any needed adjustments to the plan. While there are many different versions of problem solving, the one that we present has six steps that are common to most, if not all problem-solving approaches.

Step 1. Identify the Problem to Be Solved

Most problems that people face are likely to produce an emotional response (e.g., feelings of frustration, fear, uncertainty, anger). Such emotional reactions can serve as a useful signal for us to pause and look around for the events that may be responsible for these feelings, keeping in mind that the events could be internal (thoughts) or external (other people). Sometimes, the event causing the problem may be obvious and other times it may be less clear. If the cause of the problem is less clear, then identifying the problem can be more difficult and it can seem vague (e.g., "I feel unhappy"). If this is the case, talking to someone such as a trusted friend or therapist, can be one way to bring the problem into sharper focus.

Step 2. Identify Your Options

In this step, you will generate a list of possible solutions to the problem; that is, what are your alternatives for solving the problem? List all of the different possible solutions to the problem. The focus should be on "what" to do and less on "how" to do it. Don't worry too much about "how" yet. In generating a list of alternatives or options, you will be engaged in a task called *brainstorming*. When brainstorming, the goal is to list as many alternatives as you can think of without judging or evaluating them for how effective they may or may not be. This can free up your mind to generate more options. Sometimes, even options that may appear "over the top" can hold part of the solution to the problem. Remember, even though you may come up with a few outlandish ideas, it doesn't mean that you would ever try them out. In this step, it's really about letting your mind be free to generate as many possible solutions to the problem that you can think of.

Step 3. Choose the Best Option

In determining the best course of action, your focus should be on the likelihood of actually using the strategy or solution you choose. For example, the form of the question would be "How likely is it that *[insert best option here]* will result in *[insert goal here]*?" So, for example, "How likely is it that apologizing to my friend will result in them forgiving me?" In determining the best option, you may find yourself weighing the pros and cons of each option in order to arrive at the option that will provide you with the best possible outcome that meets your goal.

Step 4. Rehearse the Option in Your Mind

After selecting the best option, rehearse the option by imagining yourself engaging in the behaviors required to effectively solve the problem. If other people are involved, imagine not only your behavior, but also their reactions to your behavior.

Then imagine how you might respond to their reactions. If you come to see that you cannot live with the possible consequences of your actions, then either modify the option or return to Step 3 and select the second-best option and repeat this step until you decide on the best option.

Step 5. Take Action

Put your plan into action. Do it all the way. If your action plan involves multiple steps, then complete each one.

Step 6. Evaluate the Outcome

Observe the consequences of your actions and ask yourself, "How effective have my actions been in solving this problem?" If you are satisfied with the outcome, then the problem-solving process is over. Congratulations, you have solved your problem! If you're not satisfied with the outcome, repeat the problem-solving process to obtain a better outcome.

Guided Imagery Exercise: Preparing for Direct Experiencing of Emotion

In previous sessions, we talked about mindfulness and how you can use it to increase your awareness of the present moment. By strengthening your attention to the present, you become more aware of the thoughts, feelings, and physical sensations that precede your decision to drink. Greater awareness of the factors that motivate your drinking can present you with opportunities to modify those factors associated with drinking in a given situation. In this session, we will bring together the mindfulness skills that you are learning with a guided imagery approach that we will be using to help you manage unpleasant emotions and uncomfortable sensations that are associated with your problem use of alcohol. We use guided imagery because it's a safe way to allow you to access the feelings and sensations without having direct and immediate access to alcohol. When imagining an unpleasant emotional situation, being mindful and accepting of any feelings that come up can help reduce the impact of those negative emotions—similar to the wave that crests and then gently washes up on the shore.

In Sessions 7–10, we'll be using something called *imaginal exposure* to help you practice managing the unpleasant emotions and sensations that are closely related to drinking for you. In preparation for these sessions, your therapist will ask you to take part in a guided imagery exercise that involves imagining yourself slicing a lemon. The goal of this lemon imagery exercise is to demonstrate how guided imagery can be used as a method for accessing our thoughts, emotions, and physical sensations.

High Risk Drinking Situations for Emotion Regulation

You and your therapist will identify and gather information about a specific drinking situation that involves uncomfortable emotions and places you at higher risk for drinking.

Making It Happen

As we said before, your therapist understands the challenges involved when learning a new behavior. Just wanting it may not be enough. Developing a plan for how to make it happen can help. However, to make it happen your plan should be realistic and specific. For example, instead of saying "I will practice mindfulness more often," it's "I am going to practice Mindful Breathing for 5 minutes at home before dinner." Keep in mind that skill practice may result in better treatment outcomes.

Between-Session Skill Practice

☐ **Dedicated Mindfulness**

(Your choice) _____ , _____ minutes, _____ times per day

Making It *Happen*: When and where? _____

Cues to remember: _____

☐ **Mindful Moments**

During: _____ , _____ times per day

Making It *Happen*: When and where? _____

Cues to remember: _____

☐ **Review what you will do to continue making progress. What specific, realistic actions could you take between now and the next session to move forward in this area?**

_____

_____

☐ **Continue building your skill set by using and rehearsing the skills whenever possible. Consider adding new or less frequently used skills in order to increase flexible use of skills.**

☐ **Complete the Daily Monitoring Log.**

☐ **Bring the workbook to your next session.**

Session Highlights

Skills Review

A menu of coping skills was provided to you in this session. Use it to develop your toolbox of skills. When you encounter a challenging situation, take time to evaluate the problem and select the tools that will help you stay sober.

Problem Solving

Most problems that people face can be addressed using a set of general problem-solving steps. The six steps outlined in this session may be applied to managing unpleasant emotions. For example, after identifying a problem (Step 1), one or more ERT skills may be identified as alternatives for solving the problem (Steps 2 and 3). Within- and between-session skill practice (Step 4) prepares you for taking action (Step 5). Finally, evaluating the outcome (Step 6) may include acceptance or flexibly choosing another adaptive ERT skill.

Direct Experiencing of Emotion

In order to understand how emotions influence alcohol use, it's important to be able to identify them and stay with them long enough to see how they exert influence over your behavior. Tolerating unpleasant emotions can be difficult, but the emotions themselves won't harm you. The goal of direct experiencing of emotion is to be able to stay with the emotion long enough to see that it changes and to know that you don't have to reflexively act to "fix it" or make it go away. During direct experiencing of emotion you will begin to see more clearly the connection between your emotions, thoughts, physical sensations, and behaviors. You will see how these experiences come and go, like ocean waves, and gain confidence in your ability to tolerate uncomfortable emotions and sensations. The key to benefitting from the direct experiencing of emotion is your openness and willingness to weaken the connection between emotions and drinking, and to learn alternative ways of responding when you experience uncomfortable thoughts, emotions, and physical sensations.

Menu of Coping Skills and Strategies

This menu of coping skills and strategies is organized by categories of what area you want to address or manage effectively. Because some skills (e.g., the mindfulness practices) are helpful for more than one category, they are listed multiple times.

Increasing Awareness

- Mindfulness skills, including Stop and Notice, Observing (watching) in the present moment, self-monitoring (Daily Monitoring Log)
- Other _____

Coping With Cravings and Urges to Drink

- Engage in mindfulness skills including Body Scan, Object-Centered Mindfulness, Mindful Breathing, and Mindful Moments.
- Watch the Wave. Slow down and observe or watch the moment-to-moment experience of craving or urge as you "ride it out."
- Eat a good meal or snack, have a nonalcoholic drink, or have something very sweet.
- Talk it through.
- Remember why. Review the benefits of not drinking and the negative consequences of drinking.
- Distract yourself or engage in positive alternate activities.
- Avoid, leave, or change the situation.
- Other _____

Managing Thoughts

- Use mindfulness skills, observing (watching from a "distance") thoughts and other present-moment experiences as they come and go, Mindful Moments, Body Scan, Object-Centered Mindfulness, and Mindful Breathing.
- Identify thoughts that may lead to drinking.
- Reappraisal. Is there another way to think about it?

- Challenge the drinking thoughts. Examples:
  For: "I'll just have one", the challenge is: "No, I can't have just one . . ."
  For: " I need a drink to relax" the challenge is: "I don't need a drink to relax, I can unwind another way."
- Self-reinforcement. Remind yourself of your successes so far. For example, usual drinking situations in which you have remained abstinent or used a new skill.
- Other _____

Managing Emotions

- Awareness skills to notice emotions in the beginning stages of their "wave."
- Watch the Wave. Slow down and observe or watch your moment-to-moment experience of emotions as you "ride them out."
- Mindfulness skills including Mindful Breathing, Mindful Moments, and Object-Centered Mindfulness.
- Take three slow breaths.
- Describe or label the emotion.
- Manage emotions with actions that can change how you're feeling.
- Reappraise your thoughts. Check your thinking to see if your thoughts are contributing to the emotions you are trying to regulate.
- Don't suppress, avoid, or escape from the emotions. If needed, take a temporary break from them (e.g., with distractions), but don't ignore what they are trying to tell you.
- Other _____
- Other _____

Drink Refusal Skills

- Say "No." Use clear, firm voice, make eye contact, and avoid vague answers and excuses.
- Suggest something else to eat, drink, or do. Change the subject.
- Ask the person to stop offering you a drink, if necessary.
- Helpful strategy: Get a nonalcoholic drink beforehand.
- Other _____

Problem Solving

- Identify the problem.
- Generate options.
- Choose the best option (short-and long-term benefits and consequences).
- Rehearse the option or plan.
- Take action.
- Evaluate the outcome and adjust, as needed.
- Other _____

Others

Use the space following to write in any additional helpful skills and strategies. They may be in a different category or specific examples of skills and strategies from the categories listed earlier.

_____

_____

_____

_____

_____

_____

Steps for Problem Solving

1. **Identify**　Identify the problem. Describe it as accurately as you can.

2. **Options**　Brainstorm as many options as possible, without ruling any out. Get creative—consider other points of view, previous successes, and what has worked for others in similar situations.

3. **Choose**　Consider your options weighing the positive, negative, short-term, and long-term effects. Then choose the best option and one backup option.

4. **Rehearse**　Rehearse the option in your mind, step by step. How will you act on your chosen option? What might you need to have in place ahead of time for it to work? Be specific. It can be helpful to write it down.

5. **Action**　Put the plan into action. Give your solution a fair trial before you evaluate it.

6. **Evaluate**　Evaluate your plan's effectiveness. Give yourself credit for aspects of your plan that were helpful. If the outcome wasn't what you wanted, consider ways to improve the plan or try another idea.

Tips for Rehearsing

- Identify the necessary steps ahead of time. For example, if doing Sudoku in a puzzle book is the best option, then you need to acquire the book, *and* have it with you *when* you need it, *including* your glasses (if you need them) and a pencil with an eraser.
- Plan how you might approach someone or what you might say.
- Put something in place to help you remember what you want to do and when you want to do it.

Problem Solving Worksheet

1. **Identify** the problem:	

2. **Options:**	Short- and long-term benefits and consequences:

3. **Choose** the best option:

4. **Rehearse**: How will you put your chosen option into use? What might you need to have in place ahead of time for it to work? When will you carry out the steps? Write out your plan step-by-step.

5. **Action**: What did you do? What was different than your original plan (if anything)?

6. **Evaluate**: How was the original problem affected? What parts were helpful? Does the plan need adjusting? Will you use it again?

Problem Solving Worksheet

1. **Identify** the problem:	
2. **Options:**	Short- and long-term benefits and consequences:
3. **Choose** the best option:	
4. **Rehearse**: How will you put your chosen option into use? What might you need to have in place ahead of time for it to work? When will you carry out the steps? Write out your plan step-by-step.	
5. **Action:** What did you do? What was different than your original plan (if anything)?	
6. **Evaluate**: How was the original problem affected? What parts were helpful? Does the plan need adjusting? Will you use it again?	

Daily Monitoring Log

Day & Date	Situation *Who, Where, When, What*	Emotion *Rate Intensity 1 to 100*	Thoughts *What thoughts were you having?*	Physical Sensations *What did you notice?*	Desire to Drink *Thought, Craving, Urge 1 to 100*	# of Drinks	Behaviors *What did you do? What skills did you use?*

Chapter 9

Session 7

Coping With a Lapse or Relapse and Direct Experiencing of Emotion

Session 7 Goals

- Identify additional situations that may increase the risk for drinking.
- Learn how to prevent a lapse or relapse.
- Prepare for direct experiencing of emotion.
- Participate in imagery exercise for managing negative emotional drinking situations.

Overview

Changing behavior may involve setbacks. For example, someone on a diet may "slip" and have a pint of ice cream, or someone who made plans to exercise in the morning may fail to get out of bed on time. When applied to drinking behavior such setbacks have been referred to as either a *lapse* or a *relapse*. A "lapse" may be thought of as the first use of alcohol following a period of abstinence, whereas a "relapse" involves continued use after the first slip (Marlatt & Gordon, 1985). But how should we define "first" use of alcohol? Is it the first sip of alcohol, the first drink, or the first day of alcohol use? To a certain degree the question, "Did you have a lapse (or relapse) this week?" will depend on your own definition of what these terms mean and whether you view your drinking behavior to have violated a personal rule or standard that you established for yourself. Although some people view drinking any amount of alcohol as a relapse, others acknowledge that a lapse is not the same as a return to a previous pattern of continuous daily heavy drinking. At the very least, a lapse implies that the person was able to stop further drinking and re-establish abstinence, whereas a relapse implies no such stopping occurred. For this reason, in the first part of today's session, we will focus our discussion on how to both prevent and cope with a lapse or relapse if one occurs. Since the approach for addressing lapses and relapse are very similar, we will use the term *relapse* to cover both types of setbacks.

In the second part of this session, your therapist will review the rationale for conducting *imaginal exposure* to a drinking situation involving unpleasant emotion and talk about why engaging with uncomfortable emotions and sensations will help.

During the imaginal exposure scenes, you and your therapist will need a way to communicate about your level of distress as well as your level of craving for alcohol. You'll develop a simple rating scale to use for this purpose. Finally, you will spend some time during this session engaged in directly experiencing the uncomfortable emotions and sensations that are related to your alcohol use. By engaging with the thoughts, feelings, and sensations associated with drinking, you will realize that these uncomfortable experiences do not last forever and that you do not need to avoid or escape them by drinking. You will also understand that your craving for alcohol in these situations decreases. The more you engage with these uncomfortable emotions, the more likely it is that the connection between these emotions and craving for alcohol becomes weaker. You will also see that you can tolerate such experiences and that you will not lose control. Importantly, you will gain confidence in your ability to manage your emotions without avoiding them by drinking. Every day, people experience distressing emotions and uncomfortable sensations such as feeling jittery, restless, or "on edge." For you, drinking in response to these uncomfortable experiences has become a way for you to escape or avoid feeling the discomfort. Like any other behavior, your drinking behavior was strengthened because, in the short-term, it reduced the uncomfortable emotions and sensations. The ultimate goal of ERT is to weaken and eventually break the connection between these uncomfortable experiences and your alcohol use.

Preventing and Coping With a Relapse

Benjamin Franklin once said that "an ounce of prevention is worth a pound of cure." Although Franklin's quote was in reference to fire safety, today, this saying is often used when referring to people's health. Recognizing that a relapse often increases the risk for negative health consequences, it is worth taking some time to think about how you might prevent a relapse from occurring. Sometimes, even the most trivial events can be disruptive to a person's ongoing sobriety. Therefore, it is important to have a plan for how to handle these situations when they arise. Although planning ahead and rehearsing a plan can go a long way towards the prevention of a relapse, changing any health-related behavior can still involve setbacks. For this reason, you and your therapist will also develop a plan for coping with a relapse should one occur.

Major Life Events and Changes

Major life events and changes associated with an increased risk for drinking can include: relationship changes or losses such as a break-up, a friend or family member moving away, a change in health for you or someone close to you, new responsibilities, work-related changes or events, or financial changes. Furthermore, life events associated with an increased risk for drinking may also be positive such as a wide-open day with no responsibilities, receiving a promotion, a graduation, a wedding, or other events that leave you feeling happy and wanting to extend or enhance that positive feeling by drinking.

- *What else might you add to this list?*
- *What events pose a greater risk for you?*

Your high-risk situations may be written on the Personal Coping Plan worksheet at the end of this chapter. When you are finished writing down your high-risk situations, you will review the Menu of Coping Skills and Strategies in Chapter 8 and select those that would be most helpful during the situations you identified.

General Coping Plan for High-Risk Situations

The "decision" to drink can occur very quickly. We put the word "decision" in quotations because people often will say that they didn't think about drinking, it just happened. They describe their behavior as automatic or happening without thought or awareness. That's the nature of habitual behaviors; the behavior (or habit) has become so strong that the person begins to act often without awareness of the factors driving the behavior. Therefore, the first action should be *no* action. STOP! TAKE A BREATH! This will interrupt the ongoing chain of events. Then leave the high-risk situation, and delay the decision to drink. Next, focus your attention on your thoughts. See if you can identify any drinking-related thoughts. If needed, you may want to review Session 4, which includes skills for managing drinking-related thoughts. Then actively manage those thoughts by challenging them, remembering the consequences of drinking and the benefits of not drinking, and reflect on the progress you have made so far. Another way to cope with difficult or high-risk situations is to make a connection to a supportive person. Think of some people who you could reach out to when you encounter a high-risk situation.

So, if you have followed the steps, you now have identified one or more situations that increase your risk for a lapse or relapse. You also have identified several drinking-related thoughts, as well as some alternatives to those thoughts. Finally, you have identified one or more alternative behaviors to drinking in that situation and some people you could call on for support. Give yourself a pat on the back. You developed your Personal Coping Plan. As you continue with your treatment, keep your coping plan handy and, just as you did here today, write down any additional situations that increase your risk for drinking and a plan for coping with them.

Back on Track: What to Do if a Relapse Occurs

Sometimes, even with the best of intentions to remain abstinent, a relapse will occur. Your reaction to a relapse can make a big difference in how quickly you are able to get back to being abstinent. For example, a relapse doesn't have to mean that you've failed, or that you have no willpower. People who blame the drinking occurrence on their own personal failing may experience a range of unpleasant emotions (e.g., guilt, shame), that can motivate further drinking as the person now attempts to escape or avoid the discomfort associated with those emotions.

Finally, people who believe that factors beyond their control (e.g., "I have no willpower") are responsible for the relapse are more likely to give in and continue drinking (i.e., turning a lapse into a relapse) than are people who view the relapse as resulting from of a specific high-risk situation.

At the end of this chapter is a general plan for what to do if a relapse occurs titled "Getting Back on Track." Your therapist will review this with you and explore the ways you can get yourself back on track if this happens to you.

Introduction to Direct Experiencing of Emotion

As we discussed previously, unpleasant emotions and physical sensations play a role in a number of unhealthy behaviors, including drinking. Many people who receive treatment for an alcohol problem report that they have a difficult time not drinking when they experience unpleasant emotions such as anger, sadness, boredom, anxiety, or frustration. In addition, many people report relapsing in situations involving unpleasant emotions and conflicts with others. Therefore, it is important to learn healthier ways of dealing with unpleasant emotions.

It is natural for people to want to escape or avoid unpleasant emotions, physical sensations, and cravings. However, problems arise when people begin to rely on alcohol as a way to cope with these uncomfortable experiences. Although avoiding these experiences may provide some relief in the short term, it actually prolongs the unpleasant emotions and cravings and can interfere with your recovery. As you may have discovered, when emotions or cravings are suppressed or pushed away, they tend to resurface or return and may become even stronger.

However, by engaging or "staying with" uncomfortable emotions, sensations, and cravings, you will notice that they often become less intense. To help you face and directly experience these uncomfortable feelings and sensations in session, we use something called *imaginal exposure*. With this technique, we will ask you to imagine going through one or more uncomfortable emotional high-risk drinking situations, in a slow, step-by-step manner. We have found that directly experiencing your unpleasant emotional situations is quite effective in reducing the intensity of your emotional responses as well as the accompanying urges and cravings. Over time, this technique can deepen your awareness and understanding of the thoughts, emotions, and sensations that occur before drinking for you. With greater awareness, you may no longer feel a need to avoid the feelings by drinking. Instead, you may become aware that such feelings are temporary, and that if you stay with them, they will pass. Finally, as you repeatedly face these situations and the intensity of your emotions and cravings decrease, your sense of self-confidence in your ability to manage these situations without drinking will increase. The ultimate goal is to enable you to experience and tolerate uncomfortable emotions, sensations, and cravings without feeling a strong need to escape or avoid by drinking or engaging in an unhealthy or harmful behavior.

Some people may say they do not experience unpleasant emotions or cravings before drinking. If this is true for you, tell your therapist. This happens from time to time and your therapist will ask you some questions about your typical or usual drinking situations. You do not have to have a specific unpleasant emotional drinking situation to benefit from this approach. All you need to identify is a situation in which you might find it difficult to abstain from drinking. Alternatively, you might identify a typical drinking situation; that is, a situation that occurs on most drinking days. It could also be a specific time of day that always seems to be associated with drinking.

Individual Distress Scale

In order to monitor changes in your level of emotion during imaginal exposure, your therapist will use a rating scale that we call the Individual Distress Scale (IDS). A rating of 0 on the IDS scale indicates no emotional distress. A rating of 100 indicates that you are extremely distressed, the most you have ever been in your life. Your therapist will work with you to develop your individual anchor points for the IDS.

Craving Scale

Your therapist also will be monitoring the intensity of your craving or urge to drink during imaginal exposure. A rating of 0 will mean that you have no craving or urge to drink at all and a rating of 100 will be the strongest craving you ever had. This is the same scale that you have been using to describe the strength of your urges and cravings on the Daily Monitoring Log.

Emotion-Related High-Risk Drinking Scene

After determining the anchor points for your emotion and craving rating scales, you will begin with an initial exposure to your chosen unpleasant emotional high-risk drinking scene. A goal for this session will be for you to become familiar with the imaginal exposure procedures and to begin the process of weakening the connection between your unpleasant emotion and your alcohol use. As you are recounting the scene, speak in the present tense (e.g., "I am reaching for the door." "I am walking up the stairs."); allow yourself to really feel the emotions, to accept them and remain in contact with them, without trying to suppress them or push them away. As you experience the emotions that go along with this scene, notice whether the intensity of the negative emotion changes, either increasing or decreasing. Also pay attention to any changes in the emotion. For example, anger may turn into guilt or sadness. If this happens, let your therapist know. You can say, "I feel sad now." Similarly, notice how the intensity of your craving for alcohol changes.

Your therapist will guide you through the scene. You will be prompted from time to time with suggestions or questions intended to obtain more details of the scene that increase how realistic the scene feels and your emotion. It's important that you do not imagine yourself drinking in the scene. If you recall, drinking can be an escape or avoidance behavior that is reinforced or strengthened when it reduces uncomfortable emotions, sensations, or cravings.

There are two ways in which the imaginal exposure can be conducted. The first way is for you to ride out the emotion and craving until they decrease on their own. By doing this, you not only realize that your emotions and cravings are temporary but you also gain confidence in your ability to accept and tolerate the discomfort without feeling a reactive need to "fix it" by drinking. The second way is to use a coping skill to bring down your level of emotion and craving. For example, when your emotion and craving ratings are at or near their peak intensity, your therapist may guide you in a Mindful Breathing exercise intended to reduce the intensity of your distress, and your urges and cravings. By doing this, you will experience firsthand how effective these coping skills can be for you. To the extent that the coping skill reduces your overall level of discomfort, the adaptive skill is strengthened and you will gain confidence in your ability to manage your unpleasant emotions and cravings when they occur.

Processing the Scene

After the imaginal exposure you will have many emotions and thoughts. For one thing, the act of slowing down and paying attention to your emotions, thoughts, sensations, and cravings can reveal a range of experiences that you were not previously aware of. Therefore, it is important to begin processing this experience with your therapist. The main goal is for you and your therapist to understand the connection between your emotions and your alcohol use.

Your therapist will ask you to describe your experience and will want to know what happened with your emotion and your craving. Was it difficult to experience the emotion? How about the craving? Were you surprised at your level of emotion and craving? Did you learn anything new about your reactions in the situation? You may also feel uncomfortable experiencing emotions you have not felt in a while. This is a common reaction and it relates to why you might want to avoid or escape such feelings—they are uncomfortable. However, you also experienced your emotion and craving changing. They are not permanent, and if you stay with the unpleasant emotions and cravings and don't push them away, the emotion changes and even decreases. You should give yourself a big pat on the back for facing these uncomfortable emotions and for seeing this through. Over time, you may begin to experience things differently. For example, you might notice that different emotions come into play or that you are more self-confident knowing that the emotion and craving can be tolerated and that they will decrease. Also, if you experienced difficulties imagining the scene or your ratings of the situation were at or below the mid-point, you and your therapist will discuss ways in which you can increase the intensity of your emotions. This may include making some changes to the scene script, discussing barriers to experiencing the emotions such as crying or being afraid of losing control, embarrassment, or shame, and concerns about drinking. If this is the case, remember that this is a safe environment in which to experience these feelings, that your therapist is comfortable with strong feelings, and that your therapist will help you develop a plan to manage any remaining urges and cravings.

Making It Happen

Developing a plan for skill practice is important. However, you also need a strategy for coping with setbacks. Practicing your skills on only two days per week instead of seven does not mean that you have blown the plan, or that you have no willpower. Accept that such setbacks are a natural part of any plan that involves a permanent change in behavior. Remind yourself that setbacks provide an opportunity to learn what went wrong. Nobody is perfect. Recommit to your plan, and get back on track.

Between-Session Skill Practice

☐ **Dedicated Mindfulness**

(Your choice) _____ , _____ minutes, _____ times per day

Making It *Happen*: When and where? _____

Cues to remember: _____

☐ **Mindful Moments**

During: _____ , _____ times per day

Making It *Happen*: When and where? _____

Cues to remember: _____

☐ **Be aware of any additional feelings related to today's imaginal exposure exercise. Note how you coped with the feelings.**
☐ **Continue to fill in the high-risk situations, coping plans, and list of supportive people in your Personal Coping Plan.**
☐ **Complete the Daily Monitoring Log.**
☐ **Bring the workbook to your next session.**

Session Highlights

Preventing and Coping With a Relapse

Some high-risk drinking situations are predictable and familiar; you encounter them on a regular basis. Other high-risk drinking situations may occur much less frequently—maybe only once! Some of these situations are unexpected, catching you unaware and unprepared, and put you at risk for a relapse. While it is difficult to prepare for the unexpected, there are a few things that you can do. First, accept that unexpected events are part of life and are unavoidable. Second, make a plan for how you will cope without drinking. Use the problem-solving method you learned in Session 6.

High-Risk Situations: General Coping Plan

No matter how much advance planning you do, chances are you will encounter high-risk situations that you haven't planned for. For these situations, it's good to have a general coping plan to fall back on when you need it. An important component of this plan is its inclusion of people who you can turn to for support.

What If I Drink?

If this happens, review the Back on Track strategies. Take steps to bring the drinking episode to an end, understand how it happened, and adjust your future plans accordingly.

Direct Experiencing of Emotion: High-Risk Drinking Scene

Emotions are temporary, and they will pass. Direct experiencing of emotion via imaginal exposure is an effective strategy for reducing the intensity of unpleasant emotions and cravings. The goal is to enable you to experience and tolerate uncomfortable emotions, sensations, and cravings without feeling a strong need to escape or avoid by drinking or engaging in an unhealthy or harmful behavior. Stay with it, learning to tolerate unpleasant emotions is a skill that gets easier with practice.

Personal Coping Plan
Major Life Events or Changes

List life events, situations, or changes (positive or negative) that could disrupt your sobriety. Then write down a coping plan for each one.

EXAMPLE *Medical emergency (of family, friend, loved one)—afterwards is highest risk for drinking.* *Watch out for crisis thoughts such as "I'm going to need a drink to calm down from this one." Challenge it: "No, I won't. Remember, this too shall pass."* *Let others know this is a high-risk time for me.* *Go straight home; don't stop. Eat, or drink water.* *Take a shower to wind down, put on sweats so I won't leave the house.* *Watch favorite shows.*

General Coping Plan

If I encounter a high-risk situation:

1. I will stop, take a breath, and bring myself to the present moment.
2. I will leave or change the situation or environment.
3. I will put off the decision to drink for 15 minutes. Cravings are temporary and I can wait them out—not drink.
4. I will manage difficult or drinking thoughts by challenging them and remembering the consequences of drinking and the benefits of not drinking. I will remind myself of my successes.
5. I will engage in distraction or other coping strategies: This may include: (use the blank space below to write down your preferred coping strategies).

_____

_____

6. I will reach out to or call supportive people:

NAME	**PHONE NUMBER**
_____	_____
_____	_____
_____	_____
_____	_____
_____	_____

Getting Back on Track

Try to remember to do the following in the event of a relapse:

1. Get rid of the alcohol and/or get away from where the drinking occurred. Remember that control is only a moment away.
2. Stop the lapse from becoming a relapse. See the lapse as a specific event rather than a "sign" that you can't have a sober lifestyle or that treatment isn't working. A drinking episode can't take away all that you have learned or your successes.
3. Make immediate plans for getting yourself back on track.
4. Get in touch with people who help you stay sober. This could be a friend, family member, or anyone else who supports your sobriety.
5. Examine the relapse openly in order to reduce the amount of guilt or shame you may feel (those thoughts can lead to a feeling of hopelessness and continued drinking).
6. Remember that a relapse is a learning experience that can help you maintain your sobriety in the long run. Analyze the triggers for the lapse. Some usual triggers are anger, frustration, stress, celebrations, alcohol cues, and testing personal control.
7. Discuss the relapse with your therapist. Together you can make a plan for lasting sobriety.
8. Examine what your expectations about drinking were at the time. That is, what did you expect or hope that drinking would do for you?
9. Renew your commitment to abstinence.
10. Make a plan for dealing with any consequences of the relapse.

FIGURE 11 Back on Track

Daily Monitoring Log

Day & Date	Situation *Who, Where, When, What*	Emotion *Rate Intensity 1 to 100*	Thoughts *What thoughts were you having?*	Physical Sensations *What did you notice?*	Desire to Drink *Thought, Craving, Urge 1 to 100*	# of Drinks	Behavior *What did you do?* *What skills did you use?*

Chapter 10

Session 8

Enhancing Social Support Networks and Direct Experiencing of Emotion

Session 8 Goals

- Explore social support network and identify social support needs.
- Continue with imagery for managing negative emotional drinking situations.

Overview

A strong social support network to turn to for help coping with life's problems can play an important role in your sobriety. Those who have a supportive social network feel more confident in their ability to achieve their treatment goals. However, people with AUD may have either failed to nourish their social support network or, due to problems related to their alcohol use, may have alienated important members of their social support network. They may feel as though they have repeatedly let these people down, making it difficult to ask for help. Furthermore, problem drinkers' social circles tend to narrow over time and include only other people who drink, making it more difficult to obtain support for quitting and increasing a person's risk for relapse following treatment. Some people may be unwilling to seek help from others because it conflicts with their view of themselves as independent. That is, they feel uncomfortable talking to others about their problems and do not like to rely upon others for help. In the first half of this session, you and your therapist will review your current social support network and identify ways to strengthen your network. You will also develop a plan for how you could comfortably make use of your network to support your treatment goals.

Also, during this session, you and your therapist will engage in the second session of imaginal exposure to an unpleasant emotion that is associated with drinking for you. Before you begin, your therapist will check in with you about any additional thoughts you may have had about your first experience with imaginal exposure. It's common for people to think about the first session of imaginal exposure between sessions. If you have any questions or concerns, either about the purpose of imaginal exposure or about your thoughts about the exposure since your last session, please share them with your therapist at this time. Sometimes people come back and want to avoid re-experiencing the uncomfortable emotions and sensations. Sometimes other strong emotions, not part of the original drinking situation, develop during ERT. Engaging with these negative emotions can trigger a desire to escape or avoid and your therapist will understand that this is a common reaction to exposure-based treatments. This is the time to remember that wanting to escape or avoid negative emotions and uncomfortable sensations is part of AUD and is related to why to you sought treatment. You were finding it difficult to manage your emotions, cravings, and physical sensations without alcohol. Remember, too, that while alcohol may reduce your discomfort in the short term, in the long run it maintains your emotions and cravings and prevents you from learning that you can tolerate such experiences, that they will decrease, and that you will remain safe and in control. Also, remember that you maintain control of your treatment. For example, with help from your therapist, you may decide to take a closer look at the imaginal scene and break it down so that you can progress at a pace that feels more manageable to you. Your therapist understands the conflict between allowing yourself to feel your emotions and keeping them bottled up. Only you can decide whether or not to feel the emotions and cravings that are connected to your alcohol use. While your therapist will encourage you to face those unpleasant experiences, they will not "push" you into facing any experiences that you are not yet ready to face. We know how difficult this can be, but we also know that people have benefited from this and similar treatment approaches used in the treatment of anxiety disorders and PTSD. So, stay engaged and make the most of your treatment experience.

Enhancing Social Support Networks

Your social supports are those people in your life—family, friends, and acquaintances—who help you cope with problems. Usually, such helping relationships are a two-way street, in that other people also gain support and help from you.

It is important for abstinent drinkers to work on building social support systems. Often in the course of a drinking career, drinkers' social circles narrow to include only other people who drink and who therefore will not be much support in efforts to quit. Also, many drinkers find it hard to ask for help from family and friends because they feel they've disappointed those who have offered support many times in the past. Those who have a network of supportive people usually feel more confident about their ability to manage their lives and are better able to cope with problems. Research has shown that people facing a personal crisis (e.g., major surgery, chronic illness, job loss, death of a loved one) do much better if they have support from the people around them.

Relationship Between Social Support and Recovery

- There are many stresses associated with problem drinking: emotional, interpersonal, financial, medical, and so on. Your chances of coping effectively are better if you have a good social support network. Staying sober, dealing with the problems that drinking has created, and managing the troublesome situations that used to trigger drinking are more difficult when a person does not have support from others.

- Often, people who stop drinking have friends who still drink or use. When you decide to stop drinking, you may feel lonely at first and miss socializing with your drinking buddies. It is especially important to begin to meet new people and to build new friendships, so that you aren't tempted to return to the bar or places you used to drink to socialize.

- Some people feel that drinking helps them socialize. They may feel uncomfortable meeting new people or socializing without drinking. Some people may avoid socializing or meeting people because it is difficult for them. This avoidance is likely to lead to loneliness, boredom, and feeling isolated, which are common high-risk situations for relapse.

- Many problem drinkers have found that their social support networks have disappeared over the years because of social withdrawal, isolation, or interpersonal conflict resulting from their alcohol use. Some people are hesitant to seek help, because it conflicts with a sense of independence or masculinity. However, a network of supportive relationships can be a good way to support sobriety.

Social Support Skill Guidelines

After you decide on a problem that you would like help with, there are three basic steps to take:

1. **Consider *what* types of support you would like.** This list may include the following:
   a. *Help with information, resources, emergency help, or problem solving.* You might need information about local clubs and community activities, apartments for rent, available jobs, small loans, shelter, needed items, transportation, and so on. This might come from someone who can expand your thinking about options and help you weigh the choices, or someone who has coped with a similar problem.
   b. *Sober friendships.* It helps to have friends with similar experiences so you can compare your reactions to theirs and have someone you can count on for support with your sobriety. Sober friends may provide you with moral support and encouragement that includes recognition and positive feedback for what you do, as well as messages of understanding, encouragement, or hope. This support can be provided without actually working on problem solving. Often, this type of social support can help you to collect information and identify resources.
   c. *Someone to share the load or help with tasks.* This may include family cooperation with household chores or help from a coworker in completing a job before a deadline.
   d. *Help with not drinking.* This can include asking your spouse to talk with you or participate in a distracting activity when you are craving, asking a friend or coworker not to offer you drinks or talk about drinking, asking a parent to handle your money for a few months so you don't have a lot of money lying around, and asking a roommate who drinks not to drink around you.
2. **Consider *who* might be helpful to you.** This list may include the following:
   a. People who are already important in your life and usually supportive of you and your sobriety.
   b. People who might potentially play a more supportive role. These may be people you know or those you don't know well yet, including an acquaintance you haven't yet approached for help, an AA member, or a relative who knows too little about your attempts to stay sober.

c. Be aware of people who are not helpful to your sobriety, even if they were helpful in the past. Some of them might become supportive, with some effort on your part. Most should be avoided.

3. **Consider *how* you can get the help you need.** The following factors help to build a social support network:

a. *Be specific.* Let the person know how they can help you. Whether you are asking for help with a task, advice, or moral support, the more specific and direct your request, the more likely you are to get the help you want.

b. *Be an active listener.* Whether you are giving support to someone else or thinking about a friend's advice about your problems, it's important to pay attention and make sure you hear accurately. Active listening includes paying attention to nonverbal behavior, not interrupting, asking questions for clarification, paraphrasing what you heard to make sure you understood, and responding to the speaker's nonverbal message, as well as to their words.

c. *Provide feedback.* Your friends and family need feedback about what was or was not helpful to you. For example, you might say, "I really appreciate your helping me think through my choices objectively, even though you have strong ideas about what I should do" or "I know you're trying to make me feel better when you say 'It'll all work out,' but it would be more helpful if you'd help me come up with some ideas for what to do." Also, remember to thank them for their support: you will be more likely to get their help again.

d. *Lend support to others.* Reliable support is a two-way street. A mutually supportive relationship is more reliable and satisfying than a situation in which one person always gives and the other always receives. Helping someone else not only benefits the recipient, but it also strengthens your own coping skills.

Adding New Sober Supports

For one reason or another, you may find that your current social support group does not provide the kind of help you need for the problem. You may be the first in your group going through a major transition, such as a commitment to sobriety. You need people who can give you an accurate picture of what to expect. You may simply wish to find a new source of moral support, a person who will understand your situation. People usually enjoy sharing their experiences, and your first request may open the door for a new friendship. For example, "Hi, we've got a mutual friend. Joe Baker tells me you've just moved into a new sober house. I need a new place to live, and the house you're in sounds great. Could we get together to talk about it so that I can decide what to do?"

Community Support Groups

Such support groups can be a valuable source of support for some people. Groups such as AA and Narcotics Anonymous (NA) have been around for many years and have helped thousands of people maintain their sobriety. Groups can be found in virtually every city across the United States and online. We recommend that a person try at least three meetings. The first few meetings can seem a bit awkward and you need to find a group that you are comfortable with. Ask your therapist to explain the many different types of groups available in your community.

Your therapist will ask you about your experience with AA and how you view AA, and will ask about your willingness to attend or your concerns about attending.

If you do not like the spiritual aspect of AA, you can try secular or nonreligious alternatives such as SOS, Rational Recovery, and SMART Recovery. All of these can be found online. If you do not have easy access to a computer, ask your therapist for help obtaining information about these programs. Of course, the decision whether or not to attend a support group is up to you.

In-Session Skill Practice: Enhancing Social Support Networks

With your therapist, begin working on the Enhancing Social Support Network worksheet. If you are uncertain about how to ask for a particular type of support, your therapist can serve as your guide and demonstrate a few options for you. Ultimately, you have to decide on an approach that is *most comfortable* for you. Notice we said "most comfortable." We understand that asking for help or support may not be easy or comfortable. If that's the case for you, please tell your therapist. They will not be surprised to hear it and can role play one or two strategies for getting the support you are looking for.

Direct Experiencing of Emotion

Reviewing Last Session's Imaginal Exposure Scene

You now have some familiarity with what it is like to engage in imaginal exposure with a personally relevant unpleasant emotional drinking situation. Although you discussed your experience with your therapist immediately after the first imaginal exposure scene, it's very common for people to have thought more about their experience between sessions. Please share your thoughts with your therapist. Some people need to be reminded of the rationale for conducting the exposures. Others want to share additional thoughts they had about their experience or their emotional reactions to the imaginal exposure scene content. If you have any concerns, please share them with your therapist. Your therapist will be able to address any concerns that may prevent you from fully participating in this session's imaginal exposure scene. Common concerns reported by clients include:

- Forgetting the reasons for conducting imaginal exposure with an unpleasant emotional drinking situation
- Experiencing unpleasant emotions (e.g., fear, shame, embarrassment) following the initial imaginal exposure session. These emotions may be related to feeling vulnerable about expressing emotions during the previous session and concerns about therapist judgment or evaluation.
- Emotions experienced during the imaginal exposure session may have "stirred up" other unpleasant emotions between sessions, thus leading one to "blame" the treatment or to be angry with the therapist.
- Discomfort with the intensity of urges and cravings during the imaginal exposure or between treatment sessions

All of these concerns can be addressed to keep you on track with your goals. Remember, your therapist's office is a safe place in which to experience the unpleasant emotions and sensations related to your urges and craving to drink. Remind yourself that emotion and cravings are not dangerous. Both emotions and cravings are temporary: They rise up, peak, and then decrease. Finally, remember the skills that you have learned in this treatment; you have the ability to manage these unpleasant experiences when they occur.

Procedures for This Exposure Session

During this imaginal exposure session—and for the next two sessions—your therapist will include information that you reported during the last session and that was associated with increases in both your level of unpleasant emotion and craving for alcohol. Just like last time, you will include as many details as you can about what you are seeing, thinking, and feeling. Because you are now familiar with how imaginal exposure works, you will have more time during this session to return to the unpleasant emotional cues that are most directly related to your alcohol use.

Your therapist will be asking you to slow things down today. This can help to further weaken the connection between your unpleasant emotions, your urges and craving to drink, and alcohol use. One way to do this is to "pause and hold" when you get to the part where your emotions are more uncomfortable. You will stay in that moment, reporting on what you see, hear, and feel, and allow time for your ratings of distress and craving to change on their own. It's like hitting the pause button when you're watching a movie. This process will deepen your awareness of uncomfortable thoughts, emotions, and sensations that precede drinking for you. With greater awareness, you may no longer feel a need to avoid these feelings by drinking. Instead, if you stay with the feelings, they will pass, and you will find that you can manage these situations without drinking. At the end of the scene, you will breathe mindfully. This will reduce any remaining distress or cravings you may have prior to ending and talking about the scene with your therapist.

Post-Exposure Processing

Just like last time, you will process the imaginal exposure with your therapist after you have finished revisiting the unpleasant emotional drinking scene at least one time. The act of slowing down and paying attention to your emotions, thoughts, physical sensations, and cravings can uncover a range of experiences that you may not have been previously aware of. You and your therapist will take a few minutes and talk about what it was like for you. Some questions to consider include:

- What was this experience like for you today?
- How was it different from the last time?
- What was it like when you paused at the uncomfortable part?
- What other emotions did you experience?
- Was anything surprising to you?
- What did you notice about the relationship between your emotion and craving?

Making It Happen

Involving other people in your social network can be a way to reach your goals. It's important to identify people who are not currently abusing substances and who are willing to support you. Engaging in a task together can help you stay motivated to complete it.

Between-Session Skill Practice

☐ **Dedicated Mindfulness**

(Your choice) _____ , _____ minutes, _____ times per day

Making It *Happen*: When and where? _____

Cues to remember: _____

☐ **Mindful Moments**

During: _____ , _____ times per day

Making It *Happen*: When and where? _____

Cues to remember: _____

☐ **Be aware of any additional feelings related to today's imaginal exposure exercise. Note how you coped with the feelings.**

☐ **Continue to fill in Enhancing Social Support Network worksheet.**

☐ **Complete the Daily Monitoring Log.**

☐ **Bring the workbook to your next session.**

Session Highlights

Enhancing Social Support

A strong social support network can play an important role in your overall well-being and sobriety. Social support is known to be beneficial for people in general, and is associated with benefits such as better physical and mental health. It may seem counterintuitive, but having a strong social support network can help you to cope with problems on your own by providing you with more self-confidence and self-worth.

As you build your social support network, remember to cast a wide net. Everyone has different strengths and you may have to seek out different relationships for different kinds of support. Support may be found at church groups, parent-teacher associations, AA meetings, senior centers, community centers, and any number of support groups.

Social support is a two-way street. An important part of maintaining a healthy social support system involves being there for other people when they need it. Take time to listen and lend a hand. In fact, we know from research that providing others with support may benefit you more than receiving support.

Direct Experiencing of Emotion: High-Risk Drinking Scene

As you continue to experience the unpleasant emotions that are associated with your drinking situations, you will deepen your awareness of uncomfortable thoughts, emotions, and sensations that precede drinking for you. With greater awareness, you may no longer feel a need to avoid these feelings by drinking. Instead, if you stay with the feelings, they will pass, and you will find that you can manage these situations without drinking.

Enhancing Social Support Networks
Guidelines

A strong social support system can strengthen your ability to achieve sobriety and can improve your overall quality of life. As you begin to strengthen your social support network, you should consider the following important factors.

What types of support would be most helpful to you?

- Help with information, emergency help, or problem solving
- Sober friendships
- Someone to share the load or help with tasks
- Help managing temptation to drink

Who might be most helpful to you?

This can include people who have been:

- Usually supportive
- Neutral, but could be more supportive, if asked
- Not helpful thus far; however, some unhelpful people could become supportive with effort

How can you get the support you need?

- Ask for what you need, being specific and direct
- Be an active listener when giving or receiving support
- Provide feedback about what is and is not helpful
- If you feel ready, thank the person for their support
- Lend your support to others
- Add new sober supports
- Community support self-help groups can be a valuable source of support. Check online for local or online support groups:

  Alcoholics Anonymous (www.aa.org)
  Narcotics Anonymous (www.na.org)
  SOS (www.sossobriety.org)
  Rational Recovery (www.rational.org)
  SMART Recovery (www.smartrecovery.org)

Enhancing Social Support Worksheet

<u>Type of Support</u>	People Who Could <u>Provide That Support</u>	<u>How Will You Go About</u> <u>Getting Support?</u>
_____	_____	_____
_____	_____	_____
_____	_____	_____
_____	_____	_____
_____	_____	_____
_____	_____	_____
_____	_____	_____
_____	_____	_____
_____	_____	_____
_____	_____	_____
_____	_____	_____
_____	_____	_____

Daily Monitoring Log

Day & Date	Situation *Who, Where, When, What*	Emotion *Rate Intensity 1 to 100*	Thoughts *What thoughts were you having?*	Physical Sensations *What did you notice?*	Desire to Drink *Thought, Craving, Urge 1 to 100*	# of Drinks	Behaviors *What did you do?* *What skills did you use?*

Chapter 11

Session 9

Seemingly Irrelevant Decisions and Direct Experiencing of Emotion

---

Session 9 Goals

- Learn about seemingly irrelevant decisions that could lead to a lapse or relapse.
- Develop a greater understanding of the role that unpleasant emotions, thoughts, and physical sensations play in influencing your drinking.
- Continue with imagery for managing negative emotional drinking situations.

Overview

Your daily life is filled with decisions. For example, if you are traveling from home to the hardware store there may be several routes you can take that are more or less equal in terms of time and distance traveled. Which route do you take? While the decision may seem small or irrelevant, a left turn at the end of your street will take you through a business district with a liquor store and two convenience stores. A right turn will take you through a residential district. Although your decision does not directly involve whether or not to drink, turning left instead of right may place you one step closer to a high-risk situation. In the first half of this session, your therapist will read you the story of SID (**S**eemingly **I**rrelevant **D**ecisions) and together you will review and discuss how the seemingly irrelevant decisions that SID made increased his risk for drinking. You will then be asked to consider how some of your day-to-day decisions may increase or decrease your risk for drinking.

During the second half of this session, you will participate in the third session of imaginal exposure to an unpleasant emotional situation that, in the past, was associated with drinking. Before you begin, your therapist will check in with you about any additional thoughts you may have had about prior imaginal exposure sessions (in Sessions 7 and 8). It's not uncommon for people to have thought about the previous sessions of imaginal exposure between sessions. If you have any questions or concerns, either about the purpose of imaginal exposure or about your thoughts about the exposure since your last session, please share them with your therapist at this time.

Seemingly Irrelevant Decisions

Your therapist will share with you the story of SID. After reading the story, you and your therapist will review SID's seemingly irrelevant decisions.

THE STORY OF SID

Vignette

Consider this story about SID*, who has an alcohol problem. Imagine him on his way home in the evening after a very long and difficult day. He should have been home hours ago. He feels achy and tired, becoming aware of his parched throat and the gnawing hunger in his stomach. He comes to a traffic light, and it turns red just in time for him to stop. Annoyed, he turns right instead of waiting. This way takes a little longer, but . . . "whatever." He notices a brightly lit sign up ahead. It's the corner store. Wasn't there something he was supposed to pick up? Yes—milk. He decides to stop and pick some up. His stomach rumbles again, reminding him to get something to eat while he's in the store. He parks and walks in, automatically turning to the left. Instantly, he sees a sign for his favorite alcoholic drink: "Buy one get one free." He turns around and walks the other way. He picks up some milk, grabs a slightly crumpled pre-made sandwich, and heads to the cash register. He remembers he has no cash and reaches for his credit card. There is a familiar face at the register. It's Gloria; she always has

---

a smile for everyone. "SID!" she exclaims, "Hey! Your favorite drink is on sale. And I saved a coupon for you—another 25% off!" He puts his items down and hesitates before he says, ". . . Oh . . . thanks, Gloria . . ." He notices the sign that states a $10 minimum is required for using a credit card. Gloria pushes the coupon toward him with an expectant smile. Debating only a second, Sid goes and gets the drinks. They are ice cold in his hands. He imagines cracking one open and taking a long drink as he sits down in his favorite chair at home. It will be the first of many that night.

SID's name is an acronym for Seemingly Irrelevant Decisions

Now that you've heard the story, you may be able to see that SID made a series of decisions that led up to his final decision to drink. At each one of these choice-points, SID could have made a different decision that would have taken him further away from a high-risk situation. Did he really have to turn right instead of waiting for the light to turn green? Did he have no alternative but to stop at *that* store, where he commonly purchased alcoholic drinks? Could he have said "no" to the coupon the cashier saved for him? Could he have purchased a candy bar instead of alcohol to put him over the $10 minimum purchase? Instead, each decision that SID made brought him one step closer to purchasing his favorite alcoholic beverage. Following are several questions for you to consider:

- What part of SID's story can you relate to?
- What other decisions could SID have made to reduce the risk of drinking?
- What coping skills could SID have used along the way? At which points?

In-Session Skill Practice: Seemingly Irrelevant Decisions

Your therapist will ask you to identify a potential high-risk drinking situation and then to consider a few of the seemingly irrelevant decisions that you might make and how each decision may either increase or decrease your risk for drinking. Along the way your therapist will prompt a discussion of possible alternative choices at each choice point.

Direct Experiencing of Emotion

The procedures for this session will be similar to the first two imaginal exposure sessions. During this imaginal exposure session, your therapist will be including cues that you reported during the last session that were associated with increases in your level of unpleasant emotion and craving for alcohol. Because you are now familiar with how imaginal exposure works, you should have more time during this session to revisit the unpleasant emotional cues that are most directly related to your alcohol use.

It's important to remember that a key part of this work is repetition. Additional practice can deepen your awareness and your ability to tolerate the uncomfortable thoughts, emotions, and sensations that occur before drinking for you. With greater awareness, you may no longer feel a need to avoid the feelings by drinking. Instead, you will experience that these feelings are temporary, and that if you stay with them, they will pass. Finally, as you repeatedly face these situations and the intensity of your emotions and cravings decrease, your sense of self-confidence in your ability to manage these situations without drinking will increase.

You and your therapist will likely go over the scene one or two more times today. However, if you feel strongly that it would be in your best interest to continue to a different scene, tell your therapist.

Whether you stay with the same unpleasant emotional drinking scene or select a new scene, remember to allow yourself to really feel the emotions, to accept them and remain in contact with them, without trying to suppress them or push them away. As you experience the emotions that go along with the scene, notice if the intensity of the emotion changes, either increasing or decreasing. Also, pay attention to any changes in the emotion. For example, anger may turn to guilt or sadness. Finally, note any changes in your urges or cravings for alcohol. Your therapist will ask you for ratings of your levels of emotion and craving every 3 to 5 minutes. You can also tell your therapist at any time when either your emotion or craving changes.

As with the previous two sessions of exposure, your therapist will be keeping track of any new information that you report that is related to increases in your level of emotion and craving. You will also be prompted from time to time with suggestions or questions that are intended to elicit more details of the scene that will increase the scene's realism and your level of emotion.

In order to derive the most benefit from this exercise, it is very important that you do not imagine yourself drinking at any point during the scene. This can lead to a decrease in your levels of emotion and craving, and it reinforces drinking as a behavior used to cope with unpleasant emotions and sensations. In ERT, emotions and cravings are viewed as waves that build, crest, and then subside naturally. When your emotions produce the strongest urges to drink, your therapist will direct you to stay in that moment, describing in detail your thoughts, emotions, and physical sensations, and reporting to your therapist when things change.

Processing the Scene

The act of slowing down and paying attention to your emotions, thoughts, sensations, and cravings can uncover a range of experiences that you may not previously have been aware of. You and your therapist will spend a few minutes talking about what it was like for you. Some questions your therapist may ask you include:

- What was the experience like for you today?
- How was it different from the last time?
- Did you learn anything new about your reactions in the situation?

If you reported that your emotion and craving changed during the scene, take this as evidence that they are not permanent but can change over time. That is, if you stay with the unpleasant emotions and cravings and don't push them away, the emotion changes and even decreases. Your therapist will also be talking with you about another way to bring out a change in your emotions: the use of a coping skill. That is, rather than waiting for your emotion to come down naturally, you will be shown how you can use an emotion regulation coping skill to decrease the intensity of both your emotion and craving.

Second Presentation of Unpleasant Emotional Drinking Scene

Time permitting, you will repeat the imaginal exposure exercise using the same scene. However, if it's clear to you and your therapist that the scene is no longer producing significant emotion or craving, then a new scene may be selected. Alternatively, you may go over the same scene again, even if the intensity of the emotion and craving is low. This is referred to as *overlearning*. Overlearning involves the repeated practice of a skill past the point of initial learning or mastery. Additional rehearsal may help you become more efficient when using a coping skill in a stressful or challenging situation. Essentially, the new skills that you have learned become second nature and require less effort to perform.

Making It Happen

Technology can be used to support your between-session skill practice. Set an alert that pops up on your cell phone or on your computer. We use the simple phrase "cue yourself," which is a way of saying that you can arrange—or rearrange—your environment to remind you to practice your skills. Low-tech methods include colorful notes that can be placed on bathroom mirrors, in cars, or on computer screens. While these reminders might seem overly simplistic or silly, they are a good way to keep the skills practice at the forefront of your mind.

Between-Session Skill Practice

☐ **Dedicated Mindfulness**

(Your choice) _____ , _____ minutes, _____ times per day

Making It *Happen*: When and where? _____

Cues to remember: _____

☐ **Mindful Moments**

During: _____ , _____ times per day

Making It *Happen*: When and where? _____

Cues to remember: _____

☐ **Be aware of any additional feelings related to today's imaginal exposure exercise. Note how you coped with the feelings.**
☐ **Complete Seemingly Irrelevant Decisions worksheet.**
☐ **Complete the Daily Monitoring Log.**
☐ **Bring the workbook to your next session.**

Session Highlights

The Importance of Seemingly Irrelevant Decisions

During and after treatment, it is possible for you to reduce your risk for drinking by examining the day-to-day choices you make. By thinking ahead about these choices, and where each of them may lead, you can anticipate possible threats or challenges to your sobriety. At first, it may feel awkward to consider your choices so carefully, but it takes less effort over time. By paying attention to your decision-making process, you can interrupt the chain of seemingly irrelevant decisions that lead to drinking. It may be easier to stop the process earlier in the sequence, before you wind up in a high-risk situation, than later on when you are in the situation and may be experiencing a strong urge to drink. Another benefit of monitoring the choices you make is that you will be identifying certain thoughts and behavior patterns that can lead to high-risk drinking situations. Thoughts like "I haven't seen Julie in awhile; I miss getting together with the girls." or "I wonder if Loughran's Pub is still open. They had the best cheeseburgers." are thoughts that often lead to decisions that can move you closer to a high-risk situation. Such thoughts should be monitored for possible urges or thoughts about drinking. Over time, you will begin to recognize such thoughts as warnings or red flags.

Direct Experiencing of Emotion: High-Risk Drinking Scene

During the imaginal exposure, you have worked with your therapist to stay with the uncomfortable emotions, thoughts, and physical sensations at times when your urge to drink was strongest. As you repeatedly face these situations and the intensity of your emotions and cravings decrease, your sense of self-confidence in your ability to manage these situations without drinking will increase.

Seemingly Irrelevant Decisions

"Little" seemingly irrelevant decisions can move you closer to high-risk situations or relapse.

When making any decision, whether large or small, review the following:

• Consider what options you may have.
• Think ahead to the possible outcomes of each option. What positive or negative consequences can you anticipate, and what are the risks of relapse?
• Choose one that will minimize your relapse risk.
  Or
• If you decide to choose a riskier option, make a coping plan to protect your sobriety.

Between-Session Skill-Practice

Think about a recent or upcoming "little" decision. The decision could involve any aspect of your life such as your job, recreational activities, friends, or family. Identify a lower risk option and a higher risk option. For the higher risk option, make a coping plan to minimize the risk of drinking.

Decision: _____

Lower risk option: _____

Higher risk option with coping plan: _____

_____

_____

_____

_____

Some examples of Seemingly Irrelevant Decisions include whether or not to keep alcohol in the house for guests, go out to see friends, eat at a restaurant or bar, take some breaks while working, make plans for how to spend free time, tell others you have stopped drinking, or where to go for a snack.

Daily Monitoring Log

Day & Date	Situation *Who, Where, When, What*	Emotion *Rate Intensity 1 to 100*	Thoughts *What thoughts were you having?*	Physical Sensations *What did you notice?*	Desire to Drink *Thought, Craving, Urge 1 to 100*	# of Drinks	Behaviors *What did you do?* *What skills did you use?*

Chapter 12

Session 10

Progress Review, Stimulus Control Strategies, and Direct Experiencing of Emotion

Session 10 Goals

- Review treatment goals and progress.
- Develop a plan to address remaining problems or concerns.
- Learn stimulus control strategies for reducing risk for drinking.
- Continue with imagery for managing negative emotional drinking situations.

Overview

In this session, your therapist will be checking in with you regarding your progress towards meeting your treatment goals. For goals that have been met, your therapist will review with you the strategies by which you were able to produce the desired changes and the steps you will take to ensure their maintenance. For goals that have not yet been fully met, you and your therapist will discuss any barriers or obstacles to change, and use a problem-solving approach to develop a plan to address the problem area.

Next, your therapist will introduce the topic of stimulus control. Stimulus control involves making changes in your physical environment that can help reduce the temptation to drink and, by doing that, reduce the risk for drinking. You will review a list of stimulus control strategies that other people with AUD have used successfully and then have the opportunity to brainstorm several strategies that could work for you and your unique situation.

Finally, you will engage in the fourth (and final) session of imaginal exposure to unpleasant emotions associated with drinking. Before you begin, your therapist will check in with you about any additional thoughts you may have about your previous experience with imaginal exposure (in Sessions 7, 8, and 9). It's not uncommon for people to have thought about the previous sessions of imaginal exposure between sessions. If you have any questions or concerns, either about the purpose of imaginal exposure or about your thoughts about the exposure since your last session, please share them with your therapist at this time.

Review of Treatment Goals and Progress

You are nearing the end of the treatment program. Your therapist will check in with you regarding your drinking goal and progress toward that goal.

When you entered treatment, your drinking goal was _____.

How would you rate your progress towards this goal? _____.

If you haven't achieved your goal, what do you think would help you reach your goal?

_____

_____

What is your goal at this time? _____

_____

Whether you have made progress toward your goal, but still have some work to do, or you've met your goal and you want to maintain it, this point in treatment is a good time to review the skills covered thus far to see which ones have been working for you.

Skills Review

By this point in treatment, we hope that the skills you are learning are helping you manage unpleasant emotions, thoughts, and sensations that are related to your alcohol use. We hope that you are spending time each day practicing these skills, to help you with regulating your emotions. You should be practicing mindfulness every day, and if you're not, then you should be working with your therapist to identify barriers to practice so that you can get back on track. We also know that in addition to your mindfulness skills practice, having a broad range of skills that are used consistently and flexibly are associated with better alcohol treatment outcomes. Are you using only one skill? Are you using different skills in different situations? Finally, within any situation, are you able to switch to using a second skill if the first skill doesn't seem to be working? Some challenging situations may require drawing upon a number of different strategies or types of strategies and adjusting your approach throughout the situation (e.g., discontinue one strategy and choose another).

We know that practicing skills requires effort but we also know that the more you practice, the less effort it takes to complete the skill practice. The more time you can give to planning and practicing skills, the more benefit you will get out of it. In this part of the session, you and your therapist will be reviewing the skills you've learned since the beginning of treatment. The Menu of Coping Skills and Strategies in this chapter will help you develop your personalized "skills toolbox" that you can use for selecting the right skills for each type of situation, that is, it will help you "choose the right tool for the job." The overall goal is to improve your ability to respond skillfully to a wide range of challenging high-risk drinking situations.

As you review the Menu of Coping Skills and Strategies, your therapist will want to know which skills you have found most helpful and if you have any comments or questions. The skills to be reviewed are:

- Mindful Observing
- Stop and Notice
- Body Scan
- Object-Centered Mindfulness
- Self-monitoring
- Watch the Wave (also called *Urge Surfing*)
- Coping skills for managing urges and cravings (i.e., avoid people or situations, decision delay, food or nonalcoholic drink, distraction)
- Mindful Breathing
- Cognitive Reappraisal
- Drink refusal skills
- Managing emotions with actions
- Coping with a lapse or relapse
- Seeking social support

Your therapist will respond to any questions and will encourage you to "try the skills out" whenever possible. Most mindfulness skills can be practiced most anytime, anywhere. Other skills such as cognitive reappraisal and drink refusal skills may be used to prepare for upcoming high-risk situations. Finally, some skills will be used in the moment, and when you are actually experiencing a craving or emotional response. Skills to use in these situations are Watch the Wave and Managing Emotions with Actions.

Stimulus Control

Up to this point, many of the skills that you have learned require you to change some aspect of your *internal* environment (e.g., thoughts, emotions, behaviors) as a way to reduce your risk for drinking. An additional skill involves modifying or changing your *external* environment to reduce your risk for drinking. Similar to the way in which your behavior can be guided by your thoughts or emotions (i.e., internal cues), so too can your behavior be guided by cues in your environment, or "external" cues. A few obvious examples of external cues that guide behavior would be an alarm clock, a traffic light, or a fire alarm. These cues can signal you when to wake up in the morning, when to cross a busy street, or when to exit a building. We call this *stimulus control*. That's another way of saying that your behavior—say, the behavior of waking up in the morning—is under the control of the alarm clock. If your alarm clock wakes you up and you get to work on time, then your behavior of setting the alarm is reinforced.

Through a similar process of reinforcement, your alcohol use has become associated with a variety of external cues in your environment. Over time, those cues can begin to motivate a behavior such as drinking. For example, if you drank frequently while sitting in your living room watching television, you might find that you experience an urge to drink when sitting in the living room and the TV is turned on. In this example, your drinking behavior is prompted by your immediate environment, which is the living room. Other examples of external cues for drinking would be the sight of your usual alcoholic beverage, or a neon sign indicating the presence of a bar or store where alcohol may be purchased. Time can also be an external cue. Here's how that might work. Let's say that most days are very structured and Jenn has little time to take a break. When Jenn gets home, she is with her husband and children who support her abstinence and whom she spends time with in the evening. Now let's say that it's the weekend, there is no pressing work for Jenn to do in the house, and her family is spending the day at her in-laws swimming. It's almost noon and her family won't be home until late in the evening. She has 8 to 10 hours of unstructured free time. She is at a loss for what to do. She paces a bit and feels a twinge of restlessness and irritability. She thinks about having a drink. In this example, the external cue is the extended period of unstructured time and the absence of people who support her sobriety. The internal cues are the unpleasant feelings that occur in this situation and her expectations of all the positive things that will happen if she drinks (e.g., feel less restless and bored, more relaxed).

Take a few moments and give some thought to how Jenn could change her external environment to help reduce her risk for drinking. Write them down in the space provided here:

_____

_____

_____

_____

After reviewing your ideas for stimulus control, your therapist will ask you for ways in which you have changed your environment to minimize temptation and reduce your risk for drinking that you can write down on the Stimulus Control worksheet at the end of this chapter. Your therapist also will review with you other environments that you may not have considered and will review with you some creative examples of stimulus control that our previous clients have shared with us. You will see that they are tailored to fit the person's specific needs.

The goal of sharing these examples with you is to get you thinking about other ways that you can modify or change up your environments to further reduce your risk of drinking. As you review the list of Stimulus Control Strategies that follows, notice that they fall into one of three categories:

1. Adding something positive to the environment.
2. Removing something that increases risk.
3. Finding an activity that is either incompatible with drinking or adds a barrier to obtaining or drinking alcohol.

Stimulus Control Strategies

Over time, people come to associate their drinking with a number of things in their environment, such as certain situations, circumstances, events, places, people, time of day, thoughts, feelings, and so on. Most anything that has been connected with drinking for you can be thought of as a "stimulus." Because it has been associated with drinking, it can stimulate or act as a cue or "trigger" to drink.

Stimulus control strategies target these cues to change or interfere with them to reduce the risk of drinking. Sometimes this means avoiding certain circumstances and people or removing alcohol from your home. Other strategies involve adding or doing something that will interfere with drinking.

What has become associated with drinking for you? When and where do you notice an increased desire to drink? What were your usual circumstances when you drank? Then ask yourself what you could change or rearrange that would disrupt these cues, and reduce or prevent your desire to drink.

Following is a list of examples of stimulus control strategies that other people have used to modify their environment(s). On the worksheet located at the end of this chapter, you will have the chance to come up with your own examples of stimulus control.

Stimulus Control Examples

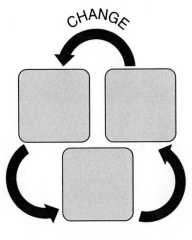

- Keep other preferred nonalcoholic beverages around.
- Keep food in the car.
- Keep healthy food at home, in car, and at work.
- Unplug the refrigerator in the garage or basement where alcohol was stored.
- Brush your teeth.
- Put jammies on (so you won't go back out again to get alcohol).
- Go late to events and leave early (it is more difficult to say "no," the longer you stay)
- Have a nephew, niece, or grandchild over when you watch football (never drink when they are around).
- Buy really good food, go overboard, and spring for the shrimp (so you don't miss alcohol as much).
- Keep a cooler of root beer in the trunk of your car for after work with co-workers.
- BYOB (nonalcoholic) to a party.
- Lock your wallet and cash in the glove compartment (so you won't go to the trouble of getting it out to buy alcohol when driving).
- Drive in the left lane (so it takes more effort to get to the liquor store exit).
- Remind yourself of goals or accomplishments.
- Make exercise clothes available at home and in the car.

- Leave gym equipment in sight and accessible (exercise is incompatible with drinking).
- Leave an unfinished puzzle on a table.
- Place pictures of family, grandkids, kids in your car and at home to remind yourself of the important people in your life.
- Keep some sweets in the car for the drive home after work if you are having physical cravings.
- Keep an AA coin in your pocket.
- Change clothing or don't change clothing at home (some people only drink in their comfortable clothing while others only drink in their work clothes).
- Call a support person (mom, partner, or friend) on way home, so you won't stop at the liquor store.
- Rearrange furniture in living room so the room feels different and there is a different vantage point.
- Keep shoes on when first getting get home and take a walk with a dog, family member, or friend.
- Plan activities for the morning after a high-risk night (usually Saturday or Sunday).
- Commit to driving.
- Drive a different way.
- Eat dinner before going home.
- Change your work schedule.
- Have a back-up show recorded on DVR to avoid channel surfing, which increases your urge to drink.

Direct Experiencing of Emotion

This is the fourth and final session in which you will be using imaginal exposure to work with unpleasant thoughts, emotions, and physical sensations that have become associated with drinking for you. You and your therapist may decide to continue using the scene from the previous session or you may decide to use a new situation. Consider choosing a new situation if your overall level of distress and craving remained low during the last exposure. If you decide to use a new situation, remember that you will have only this session in which to engage with the unpleasant emotions and cravings. That is, there may not be sufficient time in which to experience and really weaken the connection between your emotions, urges, and cravings, and drinking. You and your therapist may discuss adding one or two more sessions of exposure, if you both feel that it could benefit you. Whatever you decide, the important point is that you work collaboratively with your therapist to choose a direction for this session that you both feel will be most beneficial to you.

Review of Previous Exposure Experiences

By this point in treatment, you will likely have observed that the connection between your unpleasant emotions and your craving to drink has grown weaker. You may be aware of greater confidence in your ability to confront the situation without drinking. You also may have noticed that if you stay with the uncomfortable emotions and sensations they will eventually decrease after a short period of time. Also, the amount of time it takes for uncomfortable emotions to decrease may have become shorter with each scene repetition. These are all signs of your increased ability to accept and tolerate unpleasant emotions and sensations without feeling the need to escape or avoid them by drinking or engaging in some other unhealthy behavior.

Reminders for Engaging in Direct Experiencing of Emotion

As you engage with the uncomfortable thoughts, emotions, and physical sensations, it is important that you do not imagine yourself drinking in the scene. Even making the decision to drink at a later time (e.g., once you leave work) can provide relief from the distress and craving you experience during the imaginal scene presentation. Remember, the goal of this exercise is to deliberately bring on the emotions and sensations that increase your desire to drink. The more you can allow yourself to accept and tolerate these uncomfortable feelings within a safe context (e.g., your therapist's office), the easier it will be to break the connection between these feelings and your desire to drink.

Prior to beginning the imaginal exposure, your therapist will review the cues discussed during the previous session. At this point, you can correct any misinformation or add new content to the imagery scene. During the scene, if your emotion or craving levels are low, your therapist will ask you what it would take to increase or intensify your emotion or urge to drink. Also, your therapist will pause or hold when you get to a part where the emotions are strongest. Your therapist will say something like, "Okay, let's hold here for a moment. . . ." You will then be asked to put your thoughts and feelings into words and describe what is taking place at that moment in the scene. As your levels of emotion and craving peak and then begin to decrease, your therapist may rewind the scene and take you back to the point at which your emotional distress or craving was strongest. As we've said before, repetition is the key to weakening that connection between your emotions and drinking.

Your job will be to picture the scene as if it were really happening to you in the moment. It's important that you allow yourself to fully experience any feelings you have, remaining in contact with them, without trying to suppress them or push them away.

Processing the Negative Emotional Drinking Scene

After the imaginal exposure to your unpleasant emotion drinking situation, you will have thoughts and feelings about the experience. Your therapist will ask you several questions to help get you thinking about what happened to your emotion and craving during the scene. Some questions for you and your therapist to consider include:

- What was it like going through that situation?
- What did you notice about your emotions and craving?
- What have you noticed across the four sessions of imaginal exposure?
- Was there a change in which emotion you were feeling?
- What else did you notice?
- What, if anything, surprised you about this situation?
- What about this situation elicits such strong emotions?

Your therapist will also share their observations with you. For example, your therapist may show you how your emotion and craving ratings changed within this session. As this is the fourth imaginal exposure session, your therapist will also review how your emotion and craving ratings have changed from session to session. Also, any large decreases in your levels of emotion and craving will be reviewed. Your therapist will ask you what happened in the scene to produce the decrease. Sometimes, during the scene, people engage in certain thoughts (e.g., focus on a distracting activity) or behaviors (e.g., leave the room in the scene where the emotion reaches its peak) to decrease the amount of distress or craving they are experiencing. These are viewed as escape or avoidance behaviors and your therapist will want to know about them. Together, you and your therapist will decide if those thoughts or behaviors will be helpful to you in the long run, or if they are ineffective coping strategies that can serve to prolong your distress and your alcohol use. Finally, if your therapist instructed you to use an emotion regulation skill near the end of the scene, you will be able to evaluate the effect of that skill on both your level of emotion and craving.

Your willingness to face these unpleasant thoughts, emotions, and physical sensations is to be commended. Give yourself a pat on the back for confronting and staying with such challenging experiences. We encourage you to continue responding to these uncomfortable experiences with greater awareness rather than reacting out of habit to escape or avoid them. With continued practice, the new skills that you have learned will themselves become a healthy habit. Congratulations!

Making It Happen

Make a commitment to practice your skills every day. Consistency is important. It's also important to be flexible in your practice and use of skills. Are you using only one skill? Are you using different skills in different situations? Finally, within any given situation, are you able to switch to using a second skill if the first one doesn't seem to be working? Some challenging situations may require drawing upon a number of different skills and adjusting your approach as the situation unfolds. By practicing a variety of skills you can improve your ability to respond skillfully to a wide range of challenging high-risk situations.

Between-Session Skill Practice

☐ **Dedicated Mindfulness**

(Your choice) _____ , _____ minutes, _____ times per day

Making It *Happen*: When and where? _____

Cues to remember: _____

☐ **Mindful Moments**

During: _____ , _____ times per day

Making It *Happen*: When and where? _____

Cues to remember: _____

☐ **Be aware of any additional feelings related to today's imaginal exposure exercise. Note how you coped with the feelings.**
☐ **Complete the Stimulus Control worksheet.**
☐ **Complete the Daily Monitoring Log.**
☐ **Bring the workbook to your next session.**

Session Highlights

Stimulus Control

Over time, people come to associate their drinking with a number of things in their environment, such as certain situations, circumstances, events, places, people, time of day, thoughts, feelings, and so on. Most anything that has been connected with drinking for you can be thought as a "stimulus." Because it has been associated with drinking, it can stimulate or act as a cue or "trigger" to drink.

Stimulus-control strategies serve to target these cues to change or interfere with these cues to reduce the risk of drinking. Sometimes this means avoiding certain situations and people or removing alcohol from your home. Other strategies involve adding or doing something different that will interfere with drinking: for example, attending church service or an AA meeting at a time when you anticipate having a strong urge to drink.

What has become associated with drinking for you? When and where do you notice an increased desire to drink? What were your usual circumstances when you drink? Then ask yourself, "What could I change or rearrange that would disrupt these cues, and reduce or prevent my desire to drink?"

Direct Experiencing of Emotion: High-Risk Drinking Scene

During this session, you and your therapist reviewed how your emotion and craving ratings have changed since you began the direct experiencing of emotion sessions. By now, you likely have a deeper understanding of which emotions trigger your strongest urges or desires to drink. You have developed a greater ability to tolerate these emotions and you are aware that by staying with these emotions, your urges to drink have decreased.

Going forward, you will encounter challenging situations, including situations in which alcohol may be available. Using your mindfulness and breathing skills in the moment to watch the wave of emotion and craving can help you manage these situations without drinking.

Stimulus Control Worksheet

Use this worksheet to brainstorm your own personal Stimulus Control strategies.

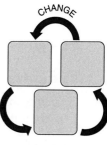

Identify problem situations or circumstances:

_____

_____

_____

_____

Identify solutions:

Be creative. To help you generate ideas, you can refer to the Stimulus Control Examples listed earlier in this chapter. To further guide you, think of things you can change or rearrange in your environment.

_____	_____
_____	_____
_____	_____
_____	_____
_____	_____
_____	_____
_____	_____
_____	_____

Updated Menu of Coping Skills and Strategies

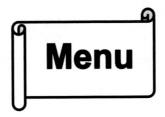

Mindfulness Skills

- Effective for awareness, managing discomfort, cravings or urges to drink, thoughts, and emotions
- Stop and Notice, Mindful Observing, Watch the Wave of cravings or urges to drink and emotions pass
- Body Scan, Object-Centered Mindfulness, Mindful Breathing, Mindful Moments and others _____

Increasing Awareness

- Self-monitoring
- Awareness of drinking-related thoughts (list of thoughts)

Coping With Cravings and Urges to Drink

- Delay the decision to act upon your urge.
- Eat a good meal or snack, have a nonalcoholic drink, or eat something very sweet.
- Talk it through.
- Remember why: Review the benefits of quitting and the negative consequences of drinking.
- Distract yourself or engage in positive alternate activities.
- Avoid, leave, or change the situation.

Managing Thoughts

- Slow things down, focus on the "here and now."
- Practice being mindful by focusing on your breathing or other activity "in the moment."

- Cognitive Reappraisal. Is there another way to think about it?
- Challenge the drinking thoughts. "No, I can't have just one. . .," "I don't need a drink to relax, I can unwind another way."
- Self-reinforcement: Remind yourself of your successes so far, such as usual drinking situations in which you have remained abstinent, used a new skill, and others.

Managing Emotions

- Slow down and observe or notice your emotions and "ride them out."
- Describe or label the emotions.
- Take three slow breaths.
- Manage emotions with actions.
- Take a temporary break from the emotions, but don't ignore or suppress them.

Problem Solving

- Identify the problem.
- Generate options and choose the best one, as well as a back-up option.
- Rehearse the plan and put it into action.
- Evaluate and adjust the plan, as needed.

Drink Refusal Skills

(Helpful strategy: Get a nonalcoholic drink beforehand.)

- Say "no." Use a clear, firm voice, make eye contact, and avoid vague answers and excuses.
- Suggest something else to eat, drink, or do. Change the subject.
- Ask the person to stop offering you a drink.
- No need to feel guilty about saying "no"; it's your right to choose what you drink.

Preventing and Coping With a Lapse

- Identify high-risk situations and develop specific coping plans ahead of time.
- Know what to do when you encounter any high-risk situation. Stop, take a breath, change the environment, manage thoughts, or distract yourself.
- If you do drink, stop the lapse from becoming a relapse. Get back on track.

Social Supports

- A good support system strengthens your sobriety. It can contribute to preventing a relapse, and getting back on track if a lapse or relapse occurs.
- Support comes in many forms including problem solving, shared sober activities, a listening ear, an extra set of hands, and specific support for staying sober.
- Self-help groups such as AA and SOS can be a valuable source of support. Rational Recovery and SMART Recovery can be found online.

Seemingly Irrelevant Decisions

- When making any decision, whether big or small, consider your options. Think ahead to the possible outcomes of each option (Benefits? Consequences? Risk of drinking?) and then choose accordingly.
- If you choose a riskier option, make a plan to protect your sobriety.

Stimulus Control Strategies

- Change or rearrange the environment.

Others

_____

_____

_____

Daily Monitoring Log

Day & Date	Situation *Who, Where, When, What*	Emotion *Rate Intensity 1 to 100*	Thoughts *What thoughts were you having?*	Physical Sensations *What did you notice?*	Desire to Drink *Thought, Craving, Urge 1 to 100*	# of Drinks	Behaviors *What did you do?* *What skills did you use?*

Chapter 13

Session 11

Relapse Prevention and Lifestyle Balance

Session 11 Goals

- Learn to identify relapse warning signs.
- Learn about lifestyle balance and its importance to relapse prevention.
- Learn about the emotion regulation strategy called *savoring* that can be used to restore lifestyle balance and enhance positive mood.

Overview

The first 3 months following treatment represent the highest risk period for relapse. Therefore, it is important that you continue to practice and use the strategies that you have learned during treatment. In the first part of this session, you and your therapist will review relapse warning signs and then develop a personalized relapse prevention plan. An important component of relapse prevention is maintaining a balanced lifestyle. Therefore, in the second part of this session you will learn how to achieve and maintain balance in your life. A component of lifestyle balance is being able to engage in behaviors that can increase your positive emotions and well-being. Your therapist will review with you strategies for cultivating positive emotions and building resources that will enhance your life satisfaction and help build endurance during times of stress.

Relapse Prevention

Relapse prevention is designed to ensure that the benefits of treatment persist well beyond the end of treatment. Following treatment, you will encounter situations or *internal* or *external* cues previously associated with alcohol use. By continuing to practice and use the skills that you have learned in treatment, you decrease the likelihood of a relapse. Practicing these strategies in different contexts will strengthen the behavior and make it more likely that you will use one or more of them in challenging situations.

Review Relapse Warning Signs

In this part of the session, you will review relapse warning signs. If you identify any warning signs, tell your therapist. In Session 12, your therapist will work with you to develop a plan to manage the increased risk for relapse. If you like, use the Menu of Coping Skills and Strategies from Session 10 of this workbook.

Relapse warning signs can be subtle such as the passage of time, or a constant low level of stress that can wear you down over time. Staying aware can take a toll as it requires self-monitoring and self-control, which requires effort and depletes your energy. However, if you let your guard down, you may become vulnerable to the subtle influence of thoughts, feelings, and behaviors associated with alcohol use. By subtle, we mean that these warning signs operate in the background, affecting our mood and behavior, but never quite grabbing our attention or rising to the level of an obvious trigger. See the list of Relapse Warning Signs at the end of this chapter.

Fortunately, subtle warning signs can be detected if you take a moment several times a day to stop what you're doing and "check-in" with yourself. "Checking-in" doesn't require much effort but it does require that you review or examine your recent thoughts, how you are feeling, and your recent behaviors. This is something that can be done at the beginning, middle, and end of each day. For example, you might ask yourself the following question: "Do I have any thoughts, behaviors, or feelings that indicate I may be vulnerable to drinking?"

It can be useful to keep track of your responses to this question on the Daily Relapse Prevention worksheet that follows. This will make those so-called subtle warning signs more obvious and easier to recognize over time. Using this worksheet, you will also be able to create a plan to manage these relapse-related thoughts, behaviors, and emotions. An extra copy of the worksheet is provided at the end of this chapter.

Daily Relapse Prevention Worksheet

Did I have any thoughts, behaviors, or feelings today that indicate that I may be vulnerable to drinking?

Mon	Tues	Wed	Thurs	Fri	Sat	Sun
☐ *Yes* ☐ *No*	☐ *Yes* ☐ *No*	☐ *Yes* ☐ *No*	☐ *Yes* ☐ *No*	☐ *Yes* ☐ *No*	☐ *Yes* ☐ *No*	☐ *Yes* ☐ *No*

If yes, list thoughts, behaviors, and feelings here:

_____

_____

_____

What could you do to reduce your risk of drinking?

_____

_____

_____

Brief List of Coping Skills
(See **Menu of Coping Skills and Strategies** from Session 10 for a more detailed list)

• Mindfulness Skills: Stop and Notice, Observe, Object-Centered Mindfulness, Body Scan, Mindful Moments	• Manage Your Emotions: Take Three Breaths, Manage emotions with actions
• Self-monitoring: Increase Awareness	• Problem solving
• Cope With Cravings: Watch the Wave (Urge Surfing)	• Drink Refusal
	• Social Support: Reach Out to Someone
• Manage Your Thoughts: Cognitive Reappraisal, Challenge Your Thoughts	• Seemingly Irrelevant Decisions: Think Ahead
	• Stimulus Control

When you identify a warning sign, Stop and Notice it, then decide if you would like to use an emotion regulation skill. In this treatment program, you have learned a new set of skills for regulating uncomfortable thoughts, emotions, and sensations. Many of the skills are practical and efficient, and can be strengthened with practice. To enhance use of these skills, practice them in different contexts and multiple times each day. As you practice each skill, it will become more automatic and require less effort. Eventually, you may say, "I don't think about being present; I am!"

Maintaining a Balanced Lifestyle

It will come as no surprise to you that people do not come equipped with an unlimited supply of energy. Much like the batteries in our electronic devices, you need to be "recharged" on a regular basis. If your battery is running low much of the time, and you never fully recharge, you might say that your lifestyle is "out of balance." However, unlike electronic devices, you do not have an easy-to-read indicator notifying you that your battery power is low. In addition, everyone is different and the things that reduce one person's "battery power" may not be the same things that reduce yours. So it's a good idea to get to know what uses and what restores your energy level.

In-Session Skill Practice: Keeping Your "Batteries" Charged

Your therapist will help you identify your personalized "low-charge" warning signs, and together you will look for ways to "recharge your battery" and restore balance to your life. You can keep track of these warning signs and recharging activities on the Lifestyle Balance Worksheet at the end of of this chapter.

Savoring

In ERT, the focus has been on managing unpleasant emotions, thoughts, and sensations. Why is this so important? It's because people consistently report that unpleasant emotions are the most common reason for relapse. However, without alcohol to create or enhance a positive feeling state, people may initially struggle with creating positive emotions. *Savoring* is an emotion regulation skill that can be used

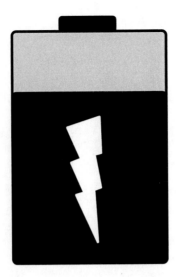

FIGURE 12 Keep Your Battery Charged

to continue and enhance a positive event or experience. There are several savoring strategies and your therapist will review them with you. Savoring strategies include directing your attention to a pleasant experience in the present moment (i.e., Mindful Moments), vividly remembering a positive past event (e.g., birth of a child, a favorite memory, the aroma of an apple pie fresh from the oven), or anticipating a future positive event (e.g., upcoming vacation), and celebrating positive events with others. Your therapist will have you select something that can be savored and that you can use for this week's Mindful Moments practice.

Making It Happen

Behaviors are strengthened if they are rewarded or reinforced. This applies to your skill practice. You can reward yourself for practicing the skills that will help you reach your goals. Notice that we are not saying reward yourself for abstinence, we are saying reward yourself for the behaviors (i.e., skills) that support or will lead to your goal of abstinence. For example, if you drink in response to unpleasant emotions, then reinforce (reward) yourself for practicing Mindful Breathing and managing emotions with action. As you strengthen these skills, you increase the likelihood of using them in high-risk drinking situations that involve unpleasant emotions. Set daily and weekly goals for skill practice and reward yourself for reaching your goals.

Between-Session Skill Practice

☐ **Dedicated Mindfulness**

Your choice _____ , _____ minutes, _____ times per day

Making It *Happen*: When and where? _____

Cues to remember: _____

☐ **Mindful Moments**

Savoring _____ , _____ times per day

Making It *Happen*: When and where? _____

Cues to remember: _____

☐ Track your responses to the daily question "Did I have any thoughts, behaviors, or feelings today that indicate I may be vulnerable to drinking?" on the Daily Relapse Prevention worksheet.

☐ Complete the Lifestyle Balance Action Plan worksheet.

☐ Complete the Daily Monitoring Log.

☐ Bring the workbook to your next session.

Session Highlights

Identifying Relapse Warning Signs

Changes in thoughts, behaviors, and emotions often occur well before a relapse. Noticing these signs provides an opportunity to intervene and prevent a return to drinking. Warning signs can be obvious or subtle, common to many people or unique to the individual. It's possible for an unwanted drinking episode to occur out of the blue with no identifiable warning signs or reasons other than the passage of time. If this is the case, acknowledge that no warning signs were evident, recommit to abstinence, and return to the sober lifestyle you've chosen for yourself.

Lifestyle Balance

An unbalanced lifestyle may pose a risk to your sobriety. For example, too many life demands can drain your energy level leaving you vulnerable to a relapse. The addition of positive lifestyle choices such as taking time to eat a well-balanced meal, leaving work on time, and getting enough sleep can help to recharge and keep your life in balance. One simple way to recharge is to savor a pleasant experience. This can be done by vividly recalling a past event or anticipating a future positive event.

Relapse Warning Signs

Changes in Thinking or Attitude

Frequency: Thoughts, urges, desires, or cravings to drink become more frequent including thoughts about "how," "where," and "when" you could drink.

Nostalgia: Fondly remembering the "good old days" when you drank and imagining it will be like that in the future.

Testing control or curiosity: "I bet I can have just one without a problem."

Crisis: "I need a few drinks to handle this one." "I went through so much, I deserve a drink."

Self-doubts: Doubting your ability to control your desire to drink or behavior of drinking. "I just have no willpower." "Trying to quit didn't work before. Why should this time be any different?"

Escape: "I just want to get away from it all" including problems, conflicts, memories, thoughts, unpleasant emotions, boredom or restlessness, sleeplessness, or low self-image.

Relaxation: "I just want to unwind—*now*" (without having to do anything else to relax). "I just need a drink to feel more at ease, more talkative, less awkward . . ." "Now that I don't drink, I'm short-tempered. Maybe it's better to be good-natured than to stop drinking right now."

To hell with it: "Why bother? What's the point?"

Other:

Behavior Changes

Health habits or daily routines: Changes in healthy, sobriety-supporting habits or routines that negatively impact quality of sleep, good nutrition, physical activity, self-care, or grooming and hygiene.

Reducing participation in sober activities: This includes self-help or counseling sessions, coping skills, or self-monitoring.

Change in social activities: Spending more time with people who drink or spending more time alone, which puts you at higher risk for drinking.

Other:

Changes in Emotions or Mood

Increase in negative mood or emotions: This can include irritability, anger, sadness, depression, anxiety, boredom, or restlessness.

Feeling stressed: You notice increases in feeling tired, worn out, run down, or unmotivated.

Other:

_____

Daily Relapse Prevention Worksheet

Did I have any thoughts, behaviors, or feelings today that indicate that I may be vulnerable to drinking?

Mon	Tues	Wed	Thurs	Fri	Sat	Sun
☐ *Yes* ☐ *No*	☐ *Yes* ☐ *No*	☐ *Yes* ☐ *No*	☐ *Yes* ☐ *No*	☐ *Yes* ☐ *No*	☐ *Yes* ☐ *No*	☐ *Yes* ☐ *No*

If yes, list thoughts, behaviors, and feelings here:

_____

_____

_____

What could you do to reduce your risk of drinking?

_____

_____

_____

Brief List of Coping Skills (See **Menu of Coping Skills and Strategies** from Session 10 for a more detailed list)	
• Mindfulness Skills: Stop and Notice, Observe, Object-Centered Mindfulness, Body Scan, Mindful Moments • Self-monitoring: Increase Awareness • Cope With Cravings: Watch the Wave (Urge Surfing) • Manage Your Thoughts: Cognitive Reappraisal, Challenge Your Thoughts	• Manage Your Emotions: Take Three Breaths, Manage emotions with actions • Problem solving • Drink Refusal • Social SupportReach Out to Someone • Seemingly Irrelevant Decisions: Think Ahead • Stimulus Control

Lifestyle Balance Worksheet

People don't have an unlimited supply of energy (unfortunately!). We need to be "recharged" on a regular basis, just like a cell phone. If our "batteries" are running low much of the time, we might say our lifestyle is "out of balance."

In order to keep your battery charged so you can carry out the choices you've made for yourself such as preventing a return to drinking, you need to know **when** it's time to use a coping skill or take some kind of action, know **what** to do, and then **Do it.**

1. **Monitor your battery.** (Know **when**)
   - Check your charge: Make it a point to Stop and Notice how you are doing each day.
   - Know the signs that you are running low.
2. **Identify some ways to increase your "charge" or energy level.** (Know **what**)
   - Is anything using too much energy? What could I change or adjust?
   - What could I add or do more of to recharge?
   - **Savoring:** An emotion regulation skill that prolongs and increases positive feelings such as being mindful of pleasant experiences as they are happening, dwelling on positive past events or anticipating future events, and sharing positive experiences with others. *What can I savor?*
3. **Choose a way to increase your charge or energy level. (Do it)**
   - What is the first step? The second step?

Signs I'm running low.

_____

_____

What uses my energy?

_____

_____

What recharges me?

_____

_____

What can I savor to make the most of my positive experiences?

_____

_____

_____

Lifestyle Balance Action Plan

Select one way to recharge in addition to savoring. Complete and carry out your Lifestyle Balance Action Plan between sessions.

Lifestyle Balance Action Plan
Select something to increase your charge, and list the steps to "make it happen".
To increase my charge or energy level, I will:
Step 1:
Step 2:
Step 3:

Daily Monitoring Log

Day & Date	Situation *Who, Where, When, What*	Emotion *Rate Intensity 1 to 100*	Thoughts *What thoughts were you having?*	Physical Sensations *What did you notice?*	Desire to Drink *Thought, Craving, Urge 1 to 100*	# of Drinks	Behavior *What did you do?* *What skills did you use?*

Chapter 14

Session 12

Accomplishments and Future Directions

Session 12 Goals

- Review your progress in treatment.
- Develop a plan for continued skill practice.
- Provide feedback to your therapist about the treatment.

Overview

In this session, you will review your progress in treatment with your therapist. The review will focus on progress towards meeting your drinking goals and on your success using the skills that you have learned in this treatment. A Relapse Prevention Plan will be completed that will include your relapse warning signs, preferred skills for managing high-risk situations, social supports, and any additional treatment needs that you and your therapist identify. You will also be given the opportunity to provide feedback on the treatment. Your opinions about the treatment program are taken seriously and will be used to change and improve the treatment for future clients.

Review of Skills

You have been introduced to many skills in this treatment program and it's important to take some time and consider those skills that have been most helpful to you, as well as identify skills that may be helpful to you in the future. Think about times during treatment when you successfully managed an urge or craving to drink or an unpleasant emotion: What worked for you? Also, as you consider life after treatment, what additional skills might you need to learn? Share your thoughts with your therapist, and if you have any questions or concerns about applying your skills after treatment, let your therapist know. As necessary, consult this workbook to remind yourself of the skills and strategies that you have used and found helpful in achieving your goals.

Review Progress Towards Drinking Goals

Your therapist will check in with you about your progress towards your drinking goals. This is similar to the reviews that were conducted in Sessions 6 and 10.
   The following questions will guide the discussion:

- *Looking back, what have you learned about your drinking triggers?*
- *What have you learned about effective methods for managing your urges and cravings for alcohol?*
- *What have you learned here that was helpful to you in making changes to your alcohol use?*
- *What will you take away from this program that will helpful in the future?*
- *Did this treatment meet your expectations? What would you want to be different?*

Review Progress With Managing Unpleasant Thoughts, Emotions, and Physical Sensations

Next, you will be asked to share your thoughts about how the treatment helped you manage your unpleasant emotions. By now, you know that unpleasant emotions are an unavoidable part of life. They provide useful information by alerting us that something in our life needs our attention. We can't get rid of them, nor should we. Attempts to avoid, suppress, or push away unpleasant emotions are not an effective long-term strategy for managing unpleasant emotions. However, we can learn more adaptive and effective ways to deal with them when they occur.

- *What have you learned about the relationship between unpleasant thoughts, emotions, and physical sensations and your use of alcohol?*
- *What have you noticed about your level of unpleasant emotions in certain situations?*
- *What have you learned that will help you face future unpleasant emotional situations?*

- *A goal of this treatment program is to help you learn effective ways to manage unpleasant thoughts, emotions, and physical sensations that are related to drinking. How effective do you think this program has been for you?*

A Return of Urges and Cravings During Times of Increased Stress

There may be times when you experience an increase in life stress. It's common during such times to experience a return of alcohol-related thoughts, unpleasant emotions, physical sensations, and urges and cravings for alcohol. This is natural and there is no cause for alarm; it doesn't mean that the effects of treatment are fading. However, it's understood that such experiences may catch you off guard. We bring it up here, because it's important to be aware that this may occur and to remember that emotions and cravings are like waves that rise up, crest, and then subside. If you find yourself in a stressful situation, and your urges and cravings return, it may be a good idea to review the material in Sessions 6 (Problem Solving) and 11 (Lifestyle Balance).

Future Plans

You and your therapist will use the Relapse Prevention Plan worksheet at the end of this chapter to discuss any current high-risk situations and your preferred skills for coping with these situations. The plan will include a list of support people that you can turn to. Finally, leaving "no stone unturned," you will troubleshoot challenging situations that you are likely to face after completing treatment.

Keep in mind that the highest risk situation (e.g., death of a parent) may not be the most likely to happen. You want to identify situations that have the potential to occur regularly in your life. Which situation or event concerns you? How would that happen? What would the situation look like? Would it jump out at you? Would it be slow to develop over time? These questions are important for helping you outline a specific plan of action. You can add the results of this discussion on your Relapse Prevention Plan.

Additional Treatment

Following treatment for an AUD, other problems may continue such as depression, anxiety, or symptoms of PTSD. If these problems were identified during your participation in ERT and they have not resolved in treatment, then your therapist may recommend seeking additional specialized treatment. Please talk with your therapist about the available options in your community. The important point is not to let these problems continue and pose a risk to your sobriety.

Feedback on Treatment

Your feedback about the treatment you have received is very valuable to us. We encourage you to tell us about the things you liked and those things that you didn't like. We can take it! Please know that the feedback we have received over the years from clients has been used to make positive changes in the treatment. We firmly believe that our clients are our best teachers. Your therapist will ask a few questions to prompt you to think about your treatment experience.

Saying Goodbye

During the course of treatment, you have worked closely with your therapist. It's very likely that you have shared important details about your life. You placed your trust in another person and learned that when dealing with unpleasant emotions the "best way out is through." Congratulations! You've worked hard in treatment and you should feel good about yourself and your accomplishments. We wish you all the best as you approach the future confident in your ability to manage life's challenging situations.

Relapse Prevention Plan

What skills, methods, and approaches have been most helpful or useful?

_____

_____

_____

_____

What are my relapse warning signs? (Identified in Session 11)

_____

_____

_____

_____

What are some high-risk situations to keep in mind?

_____

_____

_____

_____

Who can I reach out to for support? (e.g., people, self-help groups, community organizations or groups)

_____

_____

_____

_____

Any additional treatment needed at this time?

_____

_____

_____

_____

Ways to Keep Your Mindfulness Practice Going

- Attend mindfulness, meditation, or yoga classes locally. Feel free to take an introductory class more than once.
- Schedule mindfulness practice in your calendar or planner. For electronic calendars, set reminders to repeat week to week. For paper calendars and planners, use a highlighter or small adhesive labels.
- Read books on mindfulness.
- Sign up for mindfulness-related newsletters, emails, or Facebook pages, or follow groups on Twitter.
- Find an "accountability" partner. Ask someone to check in with you on a regular basis to ensure that you are practicing mindfulness. Perhaps they could help you problem solve barriers to mindfulness practice. Supportive family, friends, or a medical or mental health care provider may be a good choice.
- Use a mindfulness app on your phone, or set reminders or alarms to cue you to practice.
- Choose cues from everyday life to remind you to practice throughout the day. These could include drinking your coffee, tea, or water, washing your hands, walking through a doorway, getting in and out of your car, looking outside through a window, washing the dishes, petting your cat or dog, watching children play or sleep, and gardening or watering the plants.
- Use a visual reminder such as a sticker, sticky note, bracelet, or a polished stone in your pocket that will remind you to be mindful. Change your visual cues to something new if you stop noticing them.
- Watch videos on mindfulness (from the library, websites, or YouTube).
- On your computer, set a mindfulness website as your home page so it automatically comes up when you log on.
- Read through this workbook on a regular basis. Set it out where you will see it: put it next to your favorite chair or on your nightstand. Put a colorful or eye-catching book cover on your workbook. Put a reminder on your calendar to look through it.

Mindfulness Resources

As the value of mindfulness has become better known, the volume of materials on this topic has multiplied rapidly. To make sure you are using high quality materials, start by looking for resources associated with experts such as Jon Kabat-Zinn, Elisha Goldstein, Jack Kornfield, Saki Santorelli, Bob Stahl, Judson Brewer, and Daniel Siegal.

Many other high-quality materials are also available. These resources can come in various forms such as videos, books, podcasts, and other audio recordings. To help you decide if a recording, book, or video is truly mindfulness based, you may consider the extent to which it agrees with or supports the basic principles of mindfulness often referred to as the attitudes of mindfulness.

Video and Audio Recordings

There are many good video and audio recordings on **YouTube** (www.youtube.com), ranging in length from just a few minutes to several hours. Some videos are guided mindfulness exercises and other videos explore the many facets of mindfulness.

The Breathing Space by Jon Kabat-Zinn: A 3 Minute Exercise
9 Attitudes by Jon Kabat-Zinn (26 minutes)
Jon Kabat-Zinn—Practical Stress Reduction (15 minutes)
An Evening With Jon Kabat-Zinn (1:22 minutes)
Jon Kabat-Zinn Defines Mindfulness
STOP: A Short Mindfulness Practice by Elisha Goldstein (3:55 minutes)
3 Mindful Things to Do When You Eat by Elisha Goldstein (1:44 minutes)
3 Mindful Things to Do When You Wake Up by Elisha Goldstein (1:19 minutes)
TED also offers numerous videos on this subject: www.ted.com/talks

Books

Goldstein, E., & Stahl, B. (2010). *A mindfulness-based stress reduction workbook.* Oakland, CA: New Harbinger Publications.

Kabat-Zinn, J. (1991). *Full catastrophe living: Using the wisdom of your body and mind to face stress, pain, and illness.* New York: Random House.

Kabat-Zinn, J. (2006). *Coming to our senses: Healing ourselves and the world through mindfulness.* New York: Hyperion.

Kabat-Zinn, J. (2012). *Mindfulness for beginners: Reclaiming the present moment—and your life*. Louisville, CO: Sounds True.

Santorelli, S. (2010). *Heal thy self: Lessons on mindfulness in medicine*. Emeryville, CA: Potter/ Ten Speed/Harmony.

Websites

Center for Mindfulness in Medicine, Health Care, and Society. www.umassmed.edu/cfm/ home/index.aspx

Mindful: Taking time for what matters. www.mindful.org

References

American Psychiatric Association. (2013). *Diagnostic and statistical manual of mental disorders* (5th ed.). Washington, DC: American Psychiatric Association.

Back, S. E., Foa, E. B., Killeen, T. K., Mills, K. L., Teeson, M., Cotton, B., et al. (2015). *Concurrent treatment of PTSD and substance use disorders using prolonged exposure (COPE): Therapist guide.* New York: Oxford University Press.

Baker, T. B., Morse, E., & Sherman, J. E. (1987). The motivation to use drugs: A psycho-biological analysis of urges. In P. C. Rivers (Ed.), *The Nebraska symposium on motivation: Alcohol use and abuse* (pp. 257–323). Lincoln: University of Nebraska Press.

Barlow, D.H., Allen, L. B., & Choate, M. L. (2004). Toward a unified treatment for emotional disorders. *Behavior Therapy, 35,* 205–230.

Bien, T., & Bien, B. (2002). *Mindful recovery: a spiritual path to healing from addiction.* New York: John Wiley & Sons.

Brown, S. A., Irwin, M., & Schuckit, M. A. (1991). Changes in anxiety among abstinent male alcoholics. *Journal of Studies on Alcohol, 52,* 55–61.

Brown, S. A., & Schuckit, M. A. (1988). Changes in depression among abstinent alcoholics. *Journal of Studies on Alcohol, 49,* 412–417.

Coffey, S. F., Schumacher, J. A., Nosen, E., Littlefield, A. K., Henslee, A., Lappen, A., et al. (2016). Trauma-focused exposure therapy for chronic posttraumatic stress disorder in alcohol and drug dependent patients: A randomized clinical trial. *Psychology of Addictive Behaviors. Special Issue: Co-occurring Posttraumatic Stress and Substance Use: Emerging Research on Correlates, Mechanisms, and Treatments, 30,* 778–790.

Gross, J. J. (1998). The emerging field of emotion regulation: An integrative review. *Review of General Psychology, 2,* 271–299.

Linehan, M. M. (1993). *Skills training manual for treating borderline personality disorder.* New York: Guilford Press.

Linehan, M. M. (2015). *DBT skills training manual* (2nd ed.). New York: Guilford Press.

Marlatt, G. A., & Gordon, J. R. (Eds.) (1985). *Relapse prevention: Maintenance strategies in the treatment of addictive behaviors*. New York: Guilford Press.

Miller, W. R., & Rollnick, S. (2013). *Motivational interviewing: Helping people change* (3rd ed.). New York: Guilford Press.

Miller, W. R., Wilbourne, P. L., & Hettema, J. E. (2003). What works? A summary of alcohol treatment outcome research. In R. K. Hester & W. R. Miller (Eds.), *Handbook of alcoholism treatment approaches: Effective alternatives* (3rd ed., pp. 13–63). Boston: Allyn and Bacon.

Monti, P. M., Kadden, R. M., Rohsenow, D. J., Cooney, N. L., & Abrams, D. B. (2002). *Treating alcohol dependence: A coping skills training guide* (2nd ed.). New York: Guilford Press.

Sayers, W. M., & Sayette, M. A. (2013). Suppression on your own terms: Internally generated displays of craving suppression predict rebound effects. *Psychological Science, 24,* 1740-1746.

Sobell, L. C., Ellingstad, T. P., & Sobell, M. B. (2000). Natural recovery from alcohol and drug problems: Methodological review of the research with suggestions for future directions. *Addiction, 95,* 749–764.

Tiffany, S. T. (1990). A cognitive model of drug urges and drug use behavior: Role of automatic and nonautomatic processes. *Psychological Review, 97,* 147–168.

Torchalla, I., Nosen, L., Rostam, H., & Allen, P. (2012). Integrated treatment programs for individuals with concurrent substance use disorders and trauma experiences: A systematic review and meta-analysis. *Journal of Substance Abuse Treatment, 42,* 65–77.

Witkiewitz, K., Bowen, S., & Donovan, D. M. (2011). Moderating effects of a craving intervention on the relation between negative mood and heavy drinking following treatment for alcohol dependence. *Journal of Consulting and Clinical Psychology, 79,* 54–63.